My Hc
AND THE WIDE WORLD

Also by John Ray

Twenty-Five Years in Kashmir: Headmaster on a Mission

My Homeland
AND THE WIDE WORLD

A Life Journey Through Education,
Culture and Faith

John Ray

Signal Books
Oxford

First published in 2024 by
Signal Books Limited
36 Minster Road
Oxford OX4 1LY
www.signalbooks.co.uk

A catalogue record for this book is available from the British
Library.

ISBN 978-1-909930-87-2 Paper

Typesetting, pre-press production and cover design: Tora Kelly
Cover Images: Surrey: SuxxesPhoto/Shutterstock; Srinagar:
Mazur Travel/Shutterstock
Printed in the UK by 4Edge Ltd

Contents

PREFACE

The germ of an idea for this book was a repeated invitation to talk, in the Yorkshire village where we now live and in the neighbouring town, about my life during the Second World War. Everyone over ninety will have memories of the War. Perhaps not so many will reflect on those years in the way that I do and can still speak clearly about them. For many of today's younger English people the years 1939 to 1945 have a mythic quality about them, and not without reason. Some time ago a Dutch lady and I, fellow guests at a wedding, were discussing our times. I was feeling less than proud of the shenanigans of our political life and of England today. 'But I think we were quite good during the War,' I said. 'You were wonderful!' was her rejoinder. Indeed that was so. Are we the same metal in 2023?

Lesslie Newbigin quotes[1] a *sotto voce* remark made to him at an international conference by the person sitting beside him, an Indonesian Christian general who turned to him and 'quietly said, "the number one question of course, Bishop, is whether the West can be converted".' Newbigin, for over thirty years a missionary in India, and his friend, a leading Christian in a mainly Muslim nation, agreed that the *real* question was back here: the West. For most of my adult life I have lived among Muslims. I found Christian faith when teaching in Pakistan, then served with my wife in Indian Kashmir for twenty-five years before working with the Church of England in the Muslim diaspora of Birmingham for an even longer period. But my life has not been 'all about Muslims'.

---

1 See Lesslie Newbigin and Jock Stein, *Mission and the Crisis of Western Culture*, Handsel Booklets, 1989.

Besides 1940 there have been two other defining years in my lifetime: 1968 and 2022. In 1968, sparked off by the Paris student riots under the banner of 'freedom', we threw away our culture and our faith - or did we, as others would say, merely discard outworn deference? In 2022, in the shadows of Covid, Putin, Brexit and Climate Change, the good years ended. It was also a time of unravelling as the fruit of the 1968 revolution began to be re-examined. If we have become unhappy with where we are, how did we get here and can we get out of it? And why does the 'extreme right' appear as the new threat to the liberal consensus of my generation?

But that distant time before 1968 may be worth more than an elegiac dismissal. Among the detritus and the outdated colonial attitudes, there was much that was good which perhaps is to be recovered. I would like to think of my grandson Rob as my typical reader. He is a lecturer in philosophy, a Marxist and a young man who thinks deeply and copes well with adversity. Our age is marked by narrow bands of self-identity so that my holding Christian faith will be a 'barrier' for some, though not for Rob. If I aim for a Christian readership, it is largely to challenge the enthusiastic evangelical tribalism of those who, like us all, have to consider whether we have any reason to expect to be sheep or goats in the light of Jesus' teaching of the judgement in St Matthew's gospel.

And now in my ninety-sixth year, confronted in 'the West' and worldwide by accelerating climate change and artificial intelligence, how do we see such existential threats in the light of the eternal Gospel? We are accustomed to viewing the Gospel in the light of our current culture, but can we see how we could reverse the equation? What does it require for Christians rather to respond effectively to our own culture in the light of the Gospel? Newbigin, a prophet for our times, set down in the 1980s, in a series of talks and articles, his growing conviction of the central importance of this 'far more difficult mission' than anything he had encountered with Brahmins in India or Muslims in Birmingham. If that was true in the 1980s, how much more so today.

Hoping to re-enter the world of my youth, I tell the story, using memory, diary and surviving friends to remind me of how it all was in my teens, twenties and thirties. I am unashamedly autobiographical as I try to speak out of life as it was at the time. It is *not* a pattern for others to follow: as a young man I tested all the boundaries. Yet it has all served as preparation for what came later. Most of us who find our way into the wider world reflect on the significance of that slow emergence, if we were so blest, from the loving cocoon of family and neighbourhood. For my first thirty years, the next adventure was the great thing. At nearly ninety-six, it still is. There is an unfolding mix between 'telling the story' and the reflection on experience that I hope makes it of some value to other travellers. 'We are the pilgrims, Master. We shall go… always a little further… it may be… Beyond that last blue mountain barred with snow, Across that angry or that glimmering sea.'[2]

I started to write this soon after the shock of the death of our Queen of over seventy years, the mind full of memories of that most remarkable lady. Perhaps this is especially so for those of us who share her extraordinary generation, who were young during the War, and who wonder if ours is still the same nation. Her life, set against much that is discouraging, was in itself a summons to genuine hope to us all. Had we been a Catholic country, she might already be in train to be made a saint, with her quietly joyful faith persisting through all the tests of time.

Earlier in the week before her death she gave two forty-minute, and surely testing, interviews; first with a departing and then with a new Prime Minister. Photographs reveal a smiling, gracious lady.

2 From James Elroy Flecker, *Hassan*, Penguin, 1948.

We may wonder if, however, they tested the physical resilience of a ninety-six-year-old just a little too much. In any event the God whom she worshipped and loved decided to call his very special daughter home. Many in leadership today are Christians. Yet most of us hide it. Whether from a dislike of wearing our faith on our sleeve, silenced by the atheist presumptions of the sixties or from a well-intended but mistaken reticence in a society of many faiths, the impression is thus falsely given that personal faith is an oddity best kept silent. Perhaps our Queen's final gift to the nation can be to encourage Christians in responsible positions to hide their motivation less - and to live it out practically without any taint or implication of superiority.

Countless numbers find, at some point in the journey, that meeting Jesus is the vital clue, the basis for fruitful and expanding life lived for the common good. The 'traveller unknown' knocked at the door of my soul in 1959 when I was thirty-one, midway through a three-year teaching contract in Pakistan.

The years before then, of carefree but eventful youth, are the subject of three chapters here. Seen in long retrospect, they were all perfect preparation for what followed, first in Kashmir and then Birmingham, and that prior to ten years of reflection in old England. Thus, though the context of these chapters is now passing beyond recall, it prefigures our world. Man's story begins in the perfect garden, it ends in the celestial multicultural city. We live today in the wonderful but messy bit in between. Can we hope to clear away some of the weeds? 'Multicultural' describes one aspect of our shrunken planet. The digital age knows no frontiers. Yet 1960s multiculturalism, modern man's now faded ideology, swept the field because the Church, which should have been in the forefront of true human brother and sisterhood, had failed its test. It had, like society at large, cold shouldered the Windrush generation of the 1950s. Visibly different human beings could not so easily, it seemed, be embraced in a long dominant and settled white English culture. When the next cross-cultural challenge arrived with the Pakistani Muslims, the Church did not know what to say, and anyway few were listening. With little deep perception, the confident young urban generation threw out so much of both our culture and religion.

With hindsight, it may be that a firm base is needed to embrace the 'other'. The fortunate of the wartime generation enjoyed that base, and my story at least suggests that to enter another's world at any depth both requires and deepens one's own identity. A grassroots knowledge and love of my southern English culture and history was enriched and deepened first by admiring then marrying into that different culture and history of Scotland. More radically, growing long relationships with Punjabi, Pathan and Kashmiri people, mainly Muslim but notably also Brahmin, Sikh and Christian, helped me appreciate an enriched common humanity. All have gifts to bring to the feast! This is not a quick 'how to' approach to cross-cultural life in Birmingham. Rather it savours aspects of our country as I knew it before the deluge of the 1960s and its long aftermath. It is not all looking back. The last chapter looks at signs of hope today, and, following Newbigin the prophet, considers what directions might now be needed.

Dedication

This book is dedicated to:

(i)   Catherine, wife of sixty-two years so far; love, faith, quick thinking, courage - the only woman I know to have deflected a mob by her words.

(ii) Our grandchildren: Rob, Johnny, Matthew, Jordan, Isaac, Isabel.

(iii) Shelby Tucker in memoriam.

Shelby Tucker, who died in Oxford aged eighty-seven in February 2023, had been my friend since we met in Pakistan in 1960. He was a traveller who explored and observed across continents. As his perilous journey recounted in *Among the Insurgents* records, and - very differently - *Burma: the Curse of Independence*, serious purpose and infectious adventure can march together. The latter book, material for his address to the US National Security Council, is a standard work in Southeast Asia libraries. The former was the basis of lectures at SOAS and to the Royal Scottish Geographical Society. Shelby was a true adventurer harking back to the heroic age of discovery.

Of East Africa, with eighteen in-depth journeys over a forty-seven-year period, there is an astonishing range of subject matter, tone and narrative, ranging from hitchhiking with his equally courageous distant cousin from their marriage in Zanzibar Cathedral at the height of Nyerere's revolution, to a deeply informed study of Christian mission. A former missionary in East Africa wrote in *The Catholic Herald* (Shelby was Anglican) of his book *The Last Banana*: 'The best book about Africa I have ever read or am ever likely to read.' Shelby's understanding of the change in a single century in East Africa from witchcraft, paganism and infant sacrifice to Christianity is exemplified by his translation, with Ilona Drivdal of *Poetry and Thinking of the Chagga: a Contribution to East African Ethnology*, by Bruno Gutmann.

Shelby was a polymath, and of course so much more to his family and his neighbours in Oxford, his home base for the last forty years.

One of his last determinations was to pay the cost of this publication. I gladly take this opportunity to celebrate his memory.

ENGLAND

A Fortunate Wartime Boyhood

My father, born in 1899, and I, arriving in 1928, have kept diaries; brief, factual notes. They had gone, forgotten in cold storage for many decades of busy life. Now they have begun to come back, entry by entry, into the light. The occasion, in this Yorkshire village where Catherine and I landed in our eighties, was a long-distance mass cycle ride, sparked off by my son-in-law in the cause of raising money to restore the medieval church where he is the Vicar.

Cycling! I have hardly touched a bike since leaving Surrey for St Andrews at the age of eighteen. In Scotland, mountains quickly became my passion. The beauty, thrill and friendships formed in the companionship of the Highland hills, summer and winter, on rock, snow or ice, continued beyond student days. A surprising National Service choosing and being accepted by the Royal Marines led on to MI6 and an interesting time alongside the Russian zone of Austria in the Alpine forests of Styria, now brought to life in the *Secret War* exhibition at the Imperial War Museum. A first job, appointed for 'Mountain Expeditions and History' at Gordonstoun, after Philip and before Charles, was my pathway to the Himalayas, first in Pakistan and then Kashmir for a quarter century. Bikes not needed.

Returning to England in 1987, to (then) Pakistani Sparkbrook in Birmingham for twenty-seven years, cycling was more hazardous than any mountain. It was on moving to Hook in Yorkshire that

I began to notice ladies, some of them elderly, riding serenely on their sit-up-and-beg bikes, others carrying small children, securely cycling along separate lanes. Also squads of the young, heads down in sporting gear, causing cars to hesitate. The Tour de Yorkshire!

So my son-in-law's biking extravaganza made me think. I had done a bit of cycling a lifetime ago. In February 1939 for my eleventh birthday I was given a Raleigh bike, 26 by 1 and 3/8th wheels, no gears and costing five pounds ten and sixpence. We lived in 'happy homely Hertfordshire', where I had watched Mrs Harris, a teacher in my excellent County Primary School in Knebworth, leave school wearing plus fours on Fridays to join her husband on a tandem bike. She knew I was interested so lent me *Highways and Byways in Hertfordshire*. I at once set off to explore the ancient villages, their great houses, churches and countryside, still little affected by modernity, with more cart horses than tractors in the farms and lanes. I remember her book, because I spilled cocoa on it and had to buy and return a new one, keeping the old for many years.

Memories of the 1930s are fragmentary, but impressions remain: the surroundings of home, adventurous family holidays, whether walking in upper Swaledale or taking bikes to the Mendips, and those special Easter holidays when my mother would see me off at Paddington for a fortnight with the Cornish cousins whose father was champion blacksmith of the south west of England.

Another constant was church, which until adolescence I just accepted as part of life's framework. It was a Congregational Church, part of my father's heritage going back to John Mead Ray, a notable Suffolk pastor who had supported Wilberforce, and hosted the freed slave Olaudah Equiano in the anti-slavery movement. He had also campaigned for the repeal of the Test and Corporation Acts which barred non-Anglicans from civic life. Father continued the tradition of holding to a faith which also held fast to justice, my mother having to dissuade him from going to Spain in 1937 to support the Republican cause. On holiday in Cornwall, church, with Aunty Elsie in the robed choir and Uncle Stan a bellringer, was very different. The bells pealed out beside the rushing river at St Mawgan, adding an element of beauty and mystery. Either way faith that meant anything deeper had to pause until in my thirties I met the kind of challenge it required.

Then in September 1939 came the War. Father's office in the City, expecting bombing, quickly evacuated to an outer suburb, Kenley in Surrey. The daily journey was too much. He sold the house he had built in 1930 and on a snowy day in December, having also sold the car as petrol was not to be had, we all travelled with the removals van to a rented house near his office.

It seemed a good move, especially as my brother and I were enrolled in the nearby Caterham School. Caterham is a Congregational foundation with Wilberforce as one of its founding trustees in1811. For my brother and me it was a lovely school.

It appeared that the Directors of Father's firm, the Phoenix Assurance company, had not noticed that Kenley was also home to an RAF Fighter Command station. The War, in any case, was far away in Poland. Then, a few months later, France fell. After Dunkirk we were suddenly front line, finding that our new home was under the flight path into Kenley's runway. The Messerschmitts found out too.

My father's diary for Sunday 11 August 1940 reads:

I and boys to Ch. in the morning. Air Raid starting at 1.10pm. On the way to Post {Air Raid Warden's Concrete Post} 2 German planes flew low overhead machine gunning. Much damage to Caterham, Kenley etc.

From then on, the War, like Covid more recently, was the backdrop to life for us as for everyone: sometimes obtrusive, sometimes just background. For many it brought tragedy, for great numbers much suffering and difficulty. I was very fortunate; for me it was a time of discovery and freedom.

Father was a strong Liberal in politics as well as a firm Christian by conviction. He much admired Churchill and exclaimed on the formation of the War Cabinet in 1939, 'Winnie's back!' Each evening through the summer of 1940 the family was glued to the wireless, especially to hear Churchill's voice. We would laugh into the radio when he mocked Mussolini as a jackal, sneaking into France as the Germans took Paris on 14 June. Those of us who heard him will not forget his lines and the tone and impact of his voice, inspiring confidence and resolve: 'If the British empire and Commonwealth should last a thousand years, men will still say, this was their finest hour,' and 'Never in the field of human conflict has so much been owed by so many to so few.' For that brief period his voice was worth all the divisions we did not have. There was little time to reflect. Each day brought aerial activity and bombs not far away, often alongside our normal summer holiday life. On 17 August, Father's diary records:

> Two raids during day. Minnie and Tim in cinema on one occasion and John up a tree but got home before it ended. Air Raid during night. German bomber brought down at 3.30am in Queen's Road. Min saw it in searchlight just before.

A school friend got on his bike next morning before the scene had been cleaned up and, still alive and in touch today, says he will never forget the sight.

By that time the police had come round advising anyone

who could to move. We needed no encouragement and within a fortnight had moved five miles out into Surrey's most beautiful countryside, to the home of a civil servant who had been urgently summoned to Washington 'for the duration', on the aircraft purchasing mission.

Rabys, a solitary ancient house on the southern slope of the greensand ridge looking to the far away line of the South Downs, had already been camouflaged as a likely marker for hostile incoming planes. The lane led to two farms before it ended as a track into the woods. It was just within cycling distance to school and for the train or bus to the Kenley office.

September 1940 was sunny and the scene idyllic, as Tim and I would stand in the field beside the old timber framed house, two small boys looking up at one of the decisive battles of the world. Miniature in scale as compared to Hitler's frozen Armageddon at Stalingrad, less dramatic than el Alamein, yet if those few hundred Spitfires and Hurricanes had not prevailed, all would have been in vain. So we watched and heard the drama far above our heads: myriad vapour trails across the sky, tiny moving dots in conflict and the distant faint short rattles of machine gun fire. An emergency airfield had been quickly created from some fields just to the west of us and we would see the Spitfires, one by one in ragged line, as they urgently sought to get above the incoming enemy.

One evening at dusk the northern sky grew red. Father said, 'That will be the Docks', and later we heard many had died in one of the heaviest raids until then, the Tate & Lyle sugar refinery at the centre of it. A few nights later a faint red glow could be seen far to the south-west, and he said, 'That's Portsmouth.'

As the days shortened into October all-night alerts became the norm. Tim and I, sleeping beside each other in two small beds, would listen to the approaching rhythmic throb of Dornier or Heinkel. A surprising number of bombs were dropped into the surrounding fields, the closest bringing some plaster down. The old house shook and trembled - as did we - but was perhaps more resistant than a modern brick and concrete building. We would put our heads under the blankets when the first of a stick of HEs (high explosives) came whistling down. A shelter built among the trees at the bottom of the garden was half full of water. I think my father, with memories of 1918, reckoned that the chance of a direct hit was very small, and the windows had been covered with sticky tape against blast. Then in June 1941, when Hitler repeated Napoleon's mistake of attacking Russia, heavy raids virtually stopped. Tragedy only visited our quiet lane three years later with the doodlebugs.

The nearest our family had come to disaster was the night a basket of incendiaries came down and Mother fell while hastily carrying my little sister down the winding staircase for fear that one might land in the roof; but neither was seriously hurt. It was on that occasion when, cycling to school the next morning, I saw a farm cart shovelling up a whole load of them along the top road. I took one home and with a friend later unscrewed the detonator cap to explode it. All proper boys collected 'souvenirs'.

Meanwhile, each school day brought two five-mile rides, to school and back. In the morning I would hurry by the main road. Returning home, I would take the rough road to World's End or Viewpoint at the crest of the Downs, then either a steep lane or a steeper rough track into Holmesdale. In an area where today the M25 hurtles overhead there would be no sound apart from birdsong or perhaps a tractor. The hedgerows and fields delighted under the colours of the seasons and ever-changing sky. An alternative, Brewer's Lane, passed Pendell Court, an early sixteenth-century manor given by Henry VIII to his discarded wife, Anne of Cleves. Uphill into Bletchingley village the deeply banked lane under its giant elms housed the nests of wren and robin in spring, while primroses, violets and wood anemones proliferated. Then down the tile-hanging of High Street and another mile to the top of our lane.

I have many good memories of school and no bad ones but few are so indelibly marked as the daily journey home, ending with a whirr of wheels down Snatts Hill, as it was then named, to our ancient house.

By the end of the year a cycling diary and a larger notebook were kept, noting, as well as much else, birds seen and on what dates, their nests and eggs, and butterflies too in the same manner. Thus the cuckoo and the nightingale signalled the beginning of spring and summer.

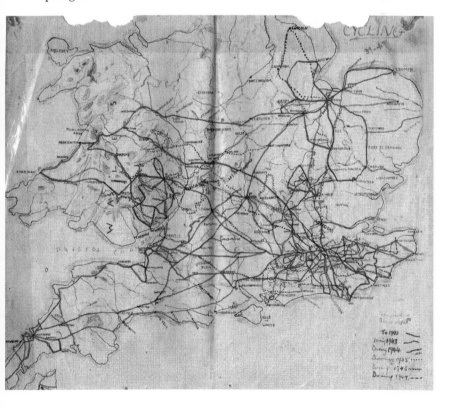

The author's hand drawn map of English cycling itineraries.

Of longer rides as I began to explore Surrey, the notebook for 1940 records: 'My second year. Handicapped badly by air raids. 5 longest 181 miles.'

The War had been relegated to being an annoying intrusion; the serious business of cycling was taking its proper place for a twelve-year-old.

Through 1941 I explored across the County and into Kent and Sussex, the quiet landscapes and old towns and villages from Guildford to Tunbridge Wells, from the North Downs and the greensand ridges across the Weald to Ashdown Forest and Hindhead. There were no signposts and even the ancient Roman milestones with the miles to London had been removed in case of invasion. I relied on a Bartholomew's ten mile to the inch pocket atlas which fitted in my back pocket.

My first ride across central London seemed nothing remarkable for a thirteen-year-old. There was little traffic even on major roads apart from buses and slow moving convoys, 'Bletchingley-Croydon-Kennington-Southwark Bridge-Strand-Knightsbridge-Putney-Wimbledon-Ewell-Banstead-Reigate-Home', with the dry comment, 'Fine. From Ewell it was dark. 61 miles.'

By 1942 a number of strategically placed aunts began to facilitate longer journeys. There was Aunty Elsie in Cornwall with a bevy of cousins, and Aunty Jessie and family, with more cousins in Weston Super Mare, and Aunty Mildred, always ready to host a young nephew, was in the Chilterns at Great Missenden. In Hereford 'Aunty' Helen was not a relation but a childhood friend of Mother. Each of these centres joined Rabys as bases from which to explore the varied regions, their peoples, history, geology and thus building styles. The needle spires of Nottinghamshire, very different from their uniquely shaped counterparts of nearby Huntingdon, point back to the proud craftsmanship of local guilds of masons. In everything from landscape to accent England was a small country of infinite variety.

In 1942 also, in aid of 'Dig for Victory', the school began five years of summer camps at Wisbech in the Fens, where an Old Boy managed a fruit farm. Staying in bell tents, picking apples and plums in fours with a ladder to each group, 'camp' run by two bachelor masters became a happy memory for many. At fourteen I was just old enough. Most went by train, but I biked there, commenting on the rough stone roads through Tottenham and staying overnight with Hugh, a friend in Hitchin, who completed the journey with me next day.

After four weeks in camp and having earned enough cash I set out alone without any idea of where I would spend the night: twenty miles against the wind to Peterborough, twenty more to Uppingham and the same again to Leicester. A lorry drivers' pull in at Fazeley on the A5 had food, but the woman said they closed on Saturday nights. Seeing my face fall she took me home with her to the house in a miners' row she shared with her daughter and her baby, bombed out from Portsmouth. Saying her husband was on late shift as she took me upstairs to a double bed she said, 'When he comes in tell him who you are.' I woke to see a man washing himself down in the corner and told him who I was. We slept, and next day she sent me off after breakfast with an orange. She must have had a brother in the Merchant Navy as we had not seen oranges or bananas for two years. By nightfall I had reached Newtown in the upper Severn Valley. People said I might get a place to sleep in the old Gro Farm where I found a few soldiers on leave with a pile of blankets. They threw me one, and next day I had the thrill, getting over the Plynlimon Pass, of looking one way to the Irish Sea and the other to Cader Idris, most beautiful of Welsh mountains. Aberystwyth produced an ample fish and chip dinner.

On the road down Cardigan Bay I was repeatedly asked for my identity card. Was it because unwelcome visitors might land from neutral Ireland across the water? The oats were still green in the fields, the country was beautiful and everyone spoke Welsh. Cardigan was full, but the Commercial Hotel had room for just one. Over supper the talk was of the War, with the armchair opinion that the new man, Montgomery, was good. It was shortly before el Alamein. Another wonderful day followed, with red squirrels, herons and buzzards for company along the wooded valley to Newcastle Emlyn, then up to Llandyssil and by a rough track over the Mynydd Epynt to Pumpsaint. Asked for directions, a group of women answered in a torrent of Welsh. Llandovery, Brecon and Hay flew past, all in sunshine along fine empty roads under the shadow of the Black Mountains. A voyage of discovery indeed!

The diary notes that I had reached Hereford on twenty-three shillings and must get home on thirty-five. First, however, came three days, well fed by Aunt Helen, exploring the county of Herefordshire, its hills and valleys, ancient 'black and white' villages and tiny remote churches. One day by contrast I dipped into industrial Wales from Bryn Mawr down the Ebbw Valley past coal mines and an iron works where I had a nasty fall and got soot in my eyes, and on to Newport, where I noted the barrage balloons protecting the harbour.

The ride home, a hundred and sixty miles, was a challenge. Thirty miles to Gloucester, then climbing from sea level to a thousand feet at Birdlip and down along the beautiful Cotswold highway past Cirencester. Near Stratton, looking on the map for a short cut over the Downs, I asked a countryman if it went to Newbury. 'Ow do I know you ain't a Jairman?' he responded. To my answer that I was just fourteen he asked, 'Ow do I know you're fourteen?' Anyway, he said it was a good road to take. So on to Newbury then Basingstoke to Farnham. By the familiar Hog's Back to Guildford, where I fixed lights. Swishing down the hill to Rabys at 10.15pm my parents were out watching for me, having phoned Helen who said I hoped to arrive about then.

In 1200 miles I had felt no risk or worry and met only natural acceptance and kindness. Quiet roads with little traffic, no mobile phones, no 'health and safety', no 'stranger danger'. England in the 1940s was for me a country of settled kindness.

This was a pattern set for the following years, with Cornwall and our closest cousins the favourite goal. It was the detail, not the long distances, that stayed in the mind: this tiny ancient church, the day's sunset or downpour, the particular youth hostel or barn. Many farmers were willing to allow a night's stay if one was not a smoker or carrying matches. Going from Wisbech to Cornwall in 1943 the diary reminds me, 'Oxford YH full, but a good meal and hay at the second farm on the Faringdon road.'

I was fortunate to have our Headmaster, Dr DGE Hall, to teach History. Formerly a professor in Rangoon he had taught some who later became independent Burma's - usually tragic - leaders. Dr Hall later resumed his academic life as Dean of South East Asian Studies at London University's School of Oriental and African Studies. For me, he opened a sense of the turning of the pages of history, of a new world struggling to be born. Such understanding was complemented by the social history teaching of Lesley Daw, Methodist lay preacher, socialist and conscientious objector. He was from Smethwick in the Black Country and challenged us in comfortable Surrey. Also special for me was the Geography teacher, Hubert Walker. I had bought his book *Walker in the Alps* and my imagination was fired by his slide shows, both of Scotland and of Switzerland.

Both in the Cotswolds and on the chalk downs the roads mainly keep to the high ground, with the villages along the streams below. In the Cotswolds one would struggle to the crest, a panoramic view now opening up to the mountains of Wales or across the Midland plain, before freewheeling down to one of the little stone towns below. In the wide open chalk country the contrast was even greater with only the prehistoric tumuli and unexplained monuments such as Silbury Hill, the Avebury Stone Circle or Stonehenge to tease the imagination, before descending to some village beside a trout stream, where the Norman church on its Saxon foundation tells of more recent waves of migration.

On these journeys I visited many of our ancient cathedrals, from stately Lincoln to Norman Peterborough and - the most perfect - Norwich. Both Exeter and Canterbury, as well as St Pauls in London, stood alone in 1942, islands in a bombed landscape.

Of course, the War had not gone away, carefree as a fortunate teenager might be. The paper map pinned to the dining room wall recounted the changing fortunes, the German advances from Warsaw nearly to Moscow, more tightly round Leningrad and Stalingrad, then all in reverse, to Berlin: equally in Africa to the gates of Cairo, then right back and slowly up the boot of Italy. A neighbour, the owner of South Park at the end of our lane, was serving there, in less mortal danger as it happened than his family at home.

In 1944 the roads were often filled with military convoys heading to the Channel coast, while the skies were full of American Flying Fortresses by day, just as the East Coast above Lincolnshire and Yorkshire was full of RAF Lancasters by night.

Soon after D Day on 6 June Father was on duty one night when he suddenly ran in, shouting, 'We've got one!' as it appeared to be a bomber on fire. But the plane continued on its course towards London. A little later - we were all awake - he called, 'We've got another!' But it was soon clear, as the enemy boasted of their secret weapon, that the V1s, the doodlebugs, were something new. Within days, standing looking east and north from the hilltop at Windy Gap above Rabys, the sky appeared to have measles as thousands of barrage balloons, in a great arc from us near the western end, round over the North Downs and circling to the

Thames estuary, shielded greater London from attack. Many got through but many were brought down in open country.

In the midst of 'Matric' examinations, we were ordered under the desks whenever one approached and passed over. One day, pushing my bike up the hill from Godstone, I heard the rackety sound approaching behind the trees to the south. Brief silence followed, then an explosion, followed by dust rising in line with Rabys. I hurried on to find the normal peaceful scene at home. Then we heard that the South Park family had been in the shelter. The mother had gone into the house briefly to make tea and was killed by a doodlebug caught by the cable of a balloon which had been set up from a base in the farmyard.

Such was the War. An amazing sequel occurred over fifty years later at a reception in Lambeth, when Catherine was talking with a lady who asked where I had lived during the War. 'In Surrey, at Bletchingley,' was her answer. Asked exactly where, she described Rabys by referring to the incident. 'I was one of the little girls in the shelter,' was the response. We have kept in touch.

VE Day followed less than a year later as did the constants of my wartime years: Caterham School, Rabys, cycling across the land, all drawing towards an end. That mirrored the nation, with demobilisation, Attlee's Labour Government and the War's logjam to change all breaking up. The country in which I had been so immersed had begun to move into a changing world.

My parents and boyhood had given me a love of adventure and a total sense of security, both personal and cultural.

Good fortune continued. With a generous Surrey County scholarship I could choose any university that would take me. I unsuccessfully tried Oxford but was accepted by St Andrews. Ten more carefree years ensued with the next adventure still my main concern. Yet serious reflection, just occasionally, began to infiltrate as - one might say - I began to grow up.

SCOTLAND

The Delectable Mountains, a Surprising National Service and Dr Hahn's School

I arrived in the little city of St Andrews with a school friend to find a bunk, as we called student lodgings. We chose one in South Street, close to the ancient, ruined cathedral. The bunkwife, Mrs Kay, fed us well and made her rules very clear to us. She was as ample as her husband was thin, in slow terminal decline having been gassed on the Western Front thirty years earlier.

Northwards we could see the line of the Angus mountains which turned white with the approach of the bitter winter of 1946. I had already been twice in mountains. The first time was during the darkest days of the War in 1941 when a family friend had taken me to the Highlands, going by overnight train from Kings Cross to Fort William. With a small tent we camped high above Glen Nevis then, when the rains had soaked both us and the tent, sought refuge in Crianlarich Youth Hostel where we met up with five young Glasgow women, and two lads with bikes, an assorted group, all walking from Dalmally beside Loch Awe in September sunshine. Never to be forgotten! On a second trip two years later, another older friend had taken two of us to the Lake District, up Striding Edge and over Helvellyn. The beauty and companionship of mountains trumped academics in my university years. Enquiries led two of us, Eric Macintyre and myself, to the Geology Department, where we learned that the Mountaineering

Club had closed when its members had gone off to war. A notice in 'cage' inviting those interested in reviving it brought forty school leavers, half of them female, to meet there. My diary for 9 February 1947 says, 'Pitlochry. To about 2000ft on Ben y Vrackie in deep snow and blizzard.' Photographs show thirty figures variously clad and shod - retreat from Moscow style.

Over Easter we were at Crianlarich Youth Hostel, then Arrochar. All beginners, with three ex-army ice axes and a length of rope, but no experience; groups climbed the frozen Ben More and the ice-sheathed Cobbler's Needle, surprisingly without accident. In a sunny June meet we luxuriated on the ridges and summits above Glencoe. October saw the return of three experienced climbers just demobilised who brought us, alarming novices, to order. The StAUMC[3] was reborn.

The Club was a nursery for us all in climbing experience and relationships. Seven years later, leading teenage boys in mountain expeditions was at the heart of my surprising first employment and remained significant into my fifties.

Tower Ridge of Ben Nevis in summer was in those days termed 'an easy day for a lady'. The Eastern Traverse is a broad grassy ledge and Tower Gap, like a deep missing tooth where the ridge narrows with a drop of a thousand feet on either side, has no terrors for any competent scrambler.

In winter it is a different matter. My diary for 15 March 1948 reads, 'left hut 10.15: Russell, JYM, Mike, Kirsty. Tower Ridge. Conditions arctic. No great diff to E Traverse - snow, ice. Through route blocked. Sensational lead to Gap. Russell leapt it (belayed). Lost axe. Summit whiteout at dusk. Down arrête, 135 degrees from top.' Those who know the terrain will appreciate the significance of that exact bearing in a frozen whiteout.

---

3 St Andrews University Mountaineering Club

Arnot Russell had climbed in the Himalaya on wartime leaves. Mike Blake had been in the Navy. JYM, Dr Macdonald, was a lecturer and member of the Scottish Mountaineering Club, while Kirsty and I were school leavers.

Two years and a lot of mountains later, in June 1950 Kirsty and I tripped from end to end of the Cuillin ridge, all its sharp three thousand-foot peaks, between 4am and 10pm. Friends had left water bottles in cairns along the route and removed the little tent we had needed in Coire Lagan. It was thought to be the first time a woman had done the circuit, but no records existed.

Relationships are in the end the mainstay of our lives. And nowhere is a better testing ground for them than the mountains, whether clothed in the extra beauty and challenge of snow and ice or in the freedom of sunlit summer days merging into each other in easily re-kindled memory. Though we later scattered to our separate lives, we will all have such recollections to our last days, part of the rich mystery of life!

Boyhood cycling had started as a solo experience but climbing is a sharing, sometimes crucially so on a hard pitch of rock, or of snow and ice. For five years every vacation and many weekends, summer and winter, were spent with a small group at the heart of the StAUMC, across the Highlands from the Cairngorms to the Cuillins. Glencoe was our Mecca, with the Youth Hostel and Clachaig Hotel, where the kindly Mr and Mrs McNiven welcomed us to tea in the parlour or for a pint in the bar. We went further, hitchhiking across France to the Alps, climbing guide-less above Chamonix and Zermatt. Eric and I, youngest of the 1949 alpine party, were not as hardened as the older members. Eric on the descent from the Matterhorn and I coming down from the Zinal Rothorn had to be helped along.

We were a mixed club, with some super girls, but exclusive relationships were not much in evidence on Club meets though at least three marriages sprang from it in those years. It was a very different culture, not one where the media suggests people hop easily into each other's beds. Are they really the better for it?

None of us *only* climbed. I ran, debated for the University and was a member of the Liberal Society. In the 1951 election we persuaded East Fife to adopt David Freeman, an urbane north Londoner, as parliamentary candidate. Speaking to small groups of venerable villagers who remembered Asquith and even Gladstone - I wonder what they made of us. 'Students!' Freeman lost his deposit but gained nearly four thousand votes. In varied ways I slowly imbibed a sense of the very different culture of the Northern Kingdom. I began to feel, often behind a severe exterior, a deep kindness, perhaps a more essentially democratic understanding of humanity. Burns' phrase 'a man's a man for a' that' sums it up. Within the rugged stone buildings, one learned, there is often a warm welcome. Was there, perhaps, less of an association with worldly power in the Scottish form of the faith than in the hierarchical associations interwoven with the Westminster establishment?

In 1947 a friend and I hitchhiked across France to an International Union of Students working party in Switzerland. We dug irrigation channels round the high pastures above Verbier and slept on straw in a cattleshed, students from around Europe all packed together. Some, like the Czechs and Hungarians, had been on the 'other side' just two years earlier. I scrambled up Mt Fort with three young Austrians who in 1944 had been in the German mountain troops on the Caucasus. America was not much trusted, and I was surprised that the Germans were not more hated, except by the French. Russia was feared by all. There was a great longing for their old Europe, so damaged by the War, physically and morally. The massive, enforced westwards transfer of populations arising from the re-drawing of frontiers in 1945, sometimes murderously executed, was something we knew little about in our cosy island. Britain was held in high regard by all, a Czech saying to me, 'You are our last hope; there is no-one else!' Student politics can be emotional, but the interplay among us was serious and genuine. Much to reflect on in 2023.

Not all was serious, and I found myself repeatedly the Jester, complete with cap and bells, in the annual Kate Kennedy Club procession round the City, I was chosen after a red gown was found one morning hanging on a washing line in the sky between the twin towers of the cathedral. I doubt if the police today would so easily accept my plea of total innocence on recovering the gown.

The classic clown is of course the other side of the unacknowledged pathos of life, and perhaps I was dimly aware of this. There was the occasion, returning from weekend climbing, when I was informed of my forthcoming execution as Bailie Foulsport. A certain Bailie Playfair of the small borough of Elie and Earlsferry had refused the students permission to collect for charity in his bailiwick, saying they were 'a perfect nuisance'. Thus, drawn from the bottle dungeon below the Castle, escorted by a piper and the kilted members of the University Training Corps, all with the tolerant approval of the Town Council, I was led to the well-constructed plinth in the crowded Market Square, arraigned by the gowned Sheriff, my soul committed by the Chaplain and caused to put my head on the executioner's block, then - only this latter part without early morning rehearsal - escaped as the University fencing club, swords drawn, stormed out of the Cross Keys Hotel. The *Scottish Daily Express* recorded and photographed my 'shinning up a drainpipe and reaching a rooftop three stories up to seek shelter through a window'. I was recaptured and duly decapitated by the hooded executioner, the severed turnip head held up to the cry of 'behold the head of a traitor' while collections for charity were duly taken from the large crowd, as well as on the approach roads to Foulsport's bailiwick. No detail was missing, with suitably dressed knitting women sitting on the straw around the plinth, *à la* French Revolution. The Baillie was duly reported as saying, 'I don't care two hoots what they do so long as it pleases them.'

The Scottish honours MA takes four years, at the end of which a Dip. Ed. gave me an excuse for another year's climbing. I ended those five years at the old grey city with qualifications for life rather different from those advertised in the University Prospectus.

A deferred National Service loomed ahead. The Royal Marines, if they would accept me, suggested an interesting alternative to the Education Corps. As recruits at the Infantry Training Centre near Exmouth we were duly licked into shape. Sergeant Buckingham, himself a Devon man, chased us round the square and made us shine our boots till they gleamed, but all with a twinkle in his eye. From the public schoolboy opposite to the Scouser on the bunk above me, we had all applied to be in the Corps, and were proud of it. To my surprise I found myself selected for officer training, then chose Commando rather than Sea Service. The Young Officers' Commando Course was vigorous, but no more so than winter days on the Highland summits.

As we gained our green berets two of us were called aside by visitors from the War Office. The Military Secretary at the Admiralty was looking for two men who knew mountains, could work alone and spoke German. Alan, an ex-Gordonstoun boy, and I were told to report in civies to an address in Vauxhall where an upstairs curtain was pulled aside as we rang the bell. MI6 requires lifelong silence, but this must be extraneous as the enterprise we were drawn into has been made fully public in the *Secret War* exhibition at the Imperial War Museum. The two of us participated in our introductory training with fascination,

CITOR

HE 'SINNED AGAINST CHARITY'

"BAILIE Ffowlsport of Wormie and Dukesford" kneels before the execution block in the market square, St. Andrews, yesterday.

BAILIE FFOWLSPORT IS 'DULY EXECUTED'

By Daily Mail Reporter

PELTED with kippers and tomatoes a "prisoner" who was alleged to have "sinned against charity" was yesterday "executed" in the market-square of St. Andrews. The victim was a student representing "Bailie Ffowlsport of Wormie and Dukesford."

The stunt was the students' reply to Bailie Playfair, of Elie and Earlsferry, who, when the Town Council refused permission to collect in the burgh, said the students were a "perfect nuisance."

When he heard about yesterday's "execution" he said : "I don't care two hoots what they do so long as it pleases them."

The sentence on the "notorious and uncharitable Bailie Ffowlsport" was carried out with the tolerant approval of St. Andrews Town Council before a large crowd as part of the charities campaign.

The prisoner was dragged from the Bottle Dungeon of St. Andrews Castle and taken in a horse-drawn cart to a scaffold in Market Street. There the sentence was read out by a "sheriff," accompanied by a "churchman" and an "executioner" dressed in black tights and close-fitting cap.

As the axe was about to fall friends of the prisoner, armed with swords, stormed the scaffold and in the confusion the prisoner escaped. Shinning up a waterpipe he clambered over roofs to a chimney-head three storeys up. He shouted defiance at the crowd, but was pursued and hauled back to the scaffold where sentence was duly carried out.

Students did not enter Elie and Earlsferry, but exacted "toll" from those entering or leaving the burgh.

More than £860 was collected up to yesterday. The aim is £1,800.

and then our time in the mountains and forests of Styria in the British zone of Austria. Our purpose was to plan and prepare for a 'Stay Behind' operation should the Russians walk in. For us it meant knowing the country in detail, selecting, mapping and monitoring sites for caches of weapons, equipment and food, and especially getting to know the keepers of the mountain huts. Skiing from hut to hut through the winter forests and sitting with Frans Filswieser beside the stove in the Lechner Haus was the icing on the cake. Almost as good were the occasions when one's turn came as courier through the Russian Zone to Vienna. At the Opera, *The Marriage of Figaro* played to a spellbound audience some of whom wore uniform: American, Russian, British or French. But the Austrians were surely saying to us from the East or the West: 'this is *our* music.' I was greatly enjoying life, a young man with the use of a Land Rover and with a Major of the Coldstream Guards, our wise and tolerant Commanding Officer in the top floor office in Klagenfurt. Perhaps our nickname in the Mess, the juvenile delinquents, contained a sliver of truth. A little tomfoolery there was an accepted part of the fun, until one morning he said to me, 'if you carry on like this, you'll always get a laugh, but no one will respect you.' I took the rebuke seriously and it marked the end of my role as a licensed jester.

National Service was coming to an end when 'they' offered me a very tempting five-year contract which would have led in a John le Carré direction. But at the vital moment a St Andrews friend teaching at Gordonstoun wrote, 'The Head wants to start mountain training here. Are you interested?' It was thus my life changing privilege to be invited for interview at Brown's hotel in Piccadilly over breakfast with Dr Hahn. As his last appointment at the school he had founded, I was taken on for 'Mountain Expeditions and History'.

In 1951, needing to expand but lacking funding to build, the school had leased a second stately home, Altyre House near Forres. Altyre, with three school houses and 120 boys, was sixteen miles from Gordonstoun. Then on Hahn's retirement joint heads were appointed, with Mr Chew, a seasoned mountaineer, at Altyre and Mr Brereton at Gordonstoun House. Seven years later the two re-joined with Chew as Head. My four years were in the middle of the Altyre period. Gordonstoun House, near the sea, had sailing. Altyre was nearer the mountains.

Set in an open space among great woods of beech and fir, the gracious Victorian mansion house was in 1953 presided over by Bobby Chew, known with affectionate respect as 'Our Father' by his staff. He had, with Geoffrey Winthrop Young, brought Hahn out of Germany in 1933 and had worked with him till the War. As Colonel Chew he had led British troops into Bergen in 1945 and had married Eva, whose first husband had died in the Norwegian resistance. Tall, regal and yet friendly and concerned, she inspired awe in us young bachelor masters whom she undertook to civilise. Most of us were in our first jobs and loved the place with its good comradeship and a lot of laughter.

I was given the old dovecot as a base for map reading, a little basic cooking, first aid, and orienteering, taking a different class of lads each week. Exercises on Dava Moor followed, intended to test and stretch the party. Small groups, dropped off at points on a desolate or gleaming moorland road after due preparation, would be given a map reference, maybe ten or twelve miles across the Moor, for pick-up sometime before dusk. In the course of the day they might chase mountain hares, plough through peat hags, face a blatter of rain, get lost and find themselves. Somehow they always reached the rendezvous, usually weary and triumphant. The trick was to judge that this particular party, with this leader, in the day's weather conditions, would all arrive.

It was the very start of 'Outdoor Education'. There were no 'qualifications' for Mountain Party leaders, no 'health and safety'. Everything hung on judgement, experience and trust. Over their school lives not a few of the boys became competent mountaineers, inured to Scottish winter conditions, exulting in the experience of days on the high tops, or basking in the sunshine in some remote glen.

Sunday was for Voluntary Expeditions. A list on the notice board would quickly fill and the school bus, a converted Army truck which the boys called the biscuit tin, would head for any of a score of marvellous mountains. We might visit the corries at the head of Glen Feshie, or the hills above Affric or Strathfarrer. With an early start Ben Nevis was within range. The plateaux of Macdhui and Braeriach were closer by. A long glissade or a tricky river crossing, the sight of an eagle or finding a raven's nest: storm and sunshine, the colouring of the seasons, the skies and the weather, made every day a new adventure. As at St Andrews, the companionship of the high hills led to friendships which continue even today.

Mr Chew soon checked up on safety. On an early November expedition into the Cairngorms John Gillespie and I, with ten fourteen-year-olds each, were staying in bothies seven miles apart. I set off next morning, but after five miles and at about three thousand feet the wind quickly turned to north-west and grew stronger, with snow coming on. We turned back and were soon brewing up in Ryvoan Bothy. I left a lad in charge and ran down most of the way to Aultnacaber where I was relieved to find John's party also back, the high plateau blotted out. A few minutes later Mr Chew arrived. Driving to a cocktail party in Nairn forty miles north he had noted the fast change in the weather. As he drove me back up the seven-mile track a relationship of trust had begun to grow. Where he had more difficulty was with the landlords whose valued shooting tenants, finding parties of boys alerting their prey at vital moments, were highly displeased.

At Altyre we were on the Highland fringe and our young English and Scottish staff relished the local scene. The feudal aristocracy provided frequent mirth. On one occasion the beaters drove the pheasants past the front of the House, where the Laird's shooting party and their attendants re-loaded their guns as waves of pheasants plummeted to the ground. Watching from the windows the boys raised a spontaneous cheer when one bird, minus a few tail feathers, finally escaped. Our landlord so loved his shooting that when the school's lease ended he pulled down the big house, returning the stones to the quarry from which they had been hewn so that his sport could resume undisturbed.

At Altyre, a young and enthusiastic staff, we felt almost a separate school compared to the assortment of older teachers, some with their German accents and peculiarities from the past, at the other establishment sixteen miles distant. Several came across to teach. One loved by all was Suzy Lachmann, a brilliant violinist and music teacher. Back in 1937 Suzy had been warned by her neighbour in Frankfurt to leave immediately. She had got on a train with her little daughter and next day phoned from the safety of London to be told, 'two gentlemen came for you an hour after you left.' Her sister Froffie, an even more acclaimed violinist, followed separately. Most of her family, like so many, were wiped out

But I had been appointed for Expeditions *and history* and so came to know the formidable figure of Dr Erich Meissner, Head of History, who in 1932 had been spirited into Switzerland from Salem to avoid arrest. I promptly bought his book *Confusion of Faces* (Faber, 1946) which traced the history of Germany from 1517 to 1939, highlighting the long struggle between religion and secularism which concluded with the total victory of the latter. I only recognised the full significance of this many years later, reflecting on my own life experience across cultures after my return from

Kashmir to England in 1986. He noted that, in a society where 'God is no longer needed', and in spite of many achievements 'rashly called progress', modern man has been the loser. 'When exposed to severe tests and luring temptations, his moral fortitude, the soundness and sanity of his mind appear to be weakened and impaired because these endowments need spiritual support which in former days religion had given and which modern secularism seems unable to provide. Christianity has been in full retreat.'

Some developments, Meissner saw, were particular to Germany, but 'the nations of Europe do not live in splendid isolation. There are deeper currents which affect them all.' He noted that Dostoevsky devotes his great imaginative powers to exploring this 'apostasy of nations', his novels revealing 'the chaos that lurks behind the petty screen of enlightened bourgeois atheism'. His vision was simple and capable of general relevance: 'The renunciation of Christ does not inaugurate enlightenment; on the contrary it invokes demons.' A great theologian was awaited to undertake what Dostoevsky attempted as an artist. Nearly a century later, in the very different setting of Europe and of Britain today, are there parallels to be drawn with the Germany of the 1920s? How well are British people prepared for severe difficulties which may be close upon us today? How many of our leaders, in Church or State, in the universities or the professions, are equipped to stand in our increasingly testing times? Many in the West in 2023 still think and act as if we were the cultural standard bearers of the world. It was Lesslie Newbigin, who after nearly forty years in India, saw as a theologian what Hahn and Meissner perceived as educationists, giving in Birmingham his last twenty years to 'that far more difficult missionary encounter', with his own collapsing culture.

Hahn, fully recovering from the breakdown that occasioned his retirement from Gordonstoun, went on to inspire and develop the Outward Bound movement and the Round Square international school network as well as, with Prince Philip, The Duke of Edinburgh's Award scheme. Under different names, these are significant today from America to Africa and from India to China. On our last visit to India in 2012 I found to my amazement our girls in Kashmir seriously working towards their expedition, craft and service sections of 'golds' for the Young People's International Award, as The Duke of Edinburgh's Award is known in that country.

Kurt Hahn came from a rich Berlin family. He had studied at Oxford before the First World War, during which he served in the German Foreign Office, becoming Private Secretary to Prince Max of Baden. In October 1918 that Christian nobleman was handed the heavy task of shouldering the burden of defeat as the last Imperial Chancellor. Prince Max took Hahn to Versailles, then in 1920, as his mentor and friend, set up Salem School with him in his Princely seat beside Lake Constance.

Schule Schloss Salem had one overall purpose: to train the young to become citizens with informed consciences, able and ready to stand firm in testing times. Through the 1920s, deep disillusionment, uncontrolled inflation and political confusion left a proud but defeated nation wide open to Hitler's promise to rebuild Germany's greatness.

Hahn's journey from Salem to Gordonstoun was occasioned by his imprisonment after openly challenging Hitler's support to young SS thugs over the grisly Potempa murder, when he called on his influential school community to break with the Nazis or break with his school. He was released and escaped to England thanks to the intervention, among others, of Ramsay MacDonald, Prime Minister in 1932.

Prince Philip had briefly been at Salem before it was taken over by the Nazis. He was then one of Gordonstoun's first pupils in 1934 becoming Head Boy in 1938. Virtually homeless and parentless on admission, the school was the nearest thing he had to 'home'. He remained close to Hahn, saying that the school had brought him 'intense happiness and excitement'. He later wrote, 'It was the mass hysteria of the Germans of those days which made Hahn so aware of the need to encourage boys to develop as responsible individuals; strong enough in mind and character to reject the standards of the mob and to resist the temptation to run with the herd.' Sir Robert Birley, then Headmaster of Eton, wrote in the foreword to the 1970 biography of Hahn, '[He] had caused many to think deeply about education, but his strength lies mainly in his determination that certain simple ideals should be put into action, above all that there must be no surrender of responsibility and no denial of the overriding claims of kindness and justice.'

In all the coverage of Prince Philip's remarkable life there was good reporting of the debt he owed to Gordonstoun, whose values of service he displayed so well. Media coverage has referred to his Headmaster as Jewish, with no mention of him as a Christian. The circumstances of his becoming one, and the spiritual thrust behind his influence, need to be better understood, if only for their relevance to our own times. In terms of the sense of grievance and bewilderment of many in Western countries today there are too many echoes of what he confronted in post-1918 Germany.

Hahn's belief that the educational system had failed to find an antidote against a poisoned civilisation will resonate with many today. He wrote, 'The system still operates as if the sources of health were still flowing from which our forebears used to benefit in their youth: the tender care of home, the brotherhood of the village or the borough, the wise guidance often experienced by the apprentice, firmly established habits of worship. Neither the love of God nor the love of man can take deep root in the unseemly haste of modern life.'

As a visionary Hahn used the compass of a school to test his ideas. Our materialist culture has seized upon the aspects of his work which it understands but has largely ignored the spiritual challenge he held out. His ideals sprang from the Cistercian model, envisaging local schools as 'islands of health' for the district. He well understood the privileged position of a private school, and always sought to see its benefits replicated in the state system. This was the 'character training' I was supposed to be involved in. The lads in the Mountain Rescue team were strong and willing and would give a good performance when called upon. But in deeper matters of character such as truthfulness, purity of intention, genuine unselfishness, I began to have an uneasy feeling that my own character was not quite exemplary.

I had come to know several of the teachers who had joined Hahn in opposing Hitler or had fled to avoid death, whether from being Jewish or simply by standing for human dignity, sometimes alone, when others hesitated from prudence or fear of retaliation. Hahn, and Gordonstoun, are sometimes critiqued on the basis of his philosophical claims or of the weaknesses and imperfections that can always be found in any large enterprise, but within his extraordinary life a main thread was the significance he gave to the individual. His blunt saying, 'character training without Christ breeds a Hitler Youth', initially offended me. It was only later that I understood its significance for Hahn in his own life journey, as well as for his school. He had early noted that the Hitler Youth had developed training in small groups at sea or in the mountains as developing qualities of initiative, determination and loyalty to 'the little platoon' - *but all without compassion*. Seeing this as a central Christian virtue was important in Hahn's own spiritual journey - he became a Christian along the way - it also led him to stress 'Samaritan service' in all his training schemes. Thus today the rescue services - the fire service, mountain rescue and coastguard watchers - continue at Gordonstoun and also in The Duke of Edinburgh's Awards and wherever Hahn's influence is seen.

In the British version of debased celebrity culture it is inevitable that Gordonstoun with its royal connections is seen as fair game to be mocked and unfairly represented as in a recent BBC television series. King Charles certainly did not share his father's uniformly joyful memories of the school, but his gratitude in certain areas of it is both on record and seen in personal documents. When I spoke in the Chapel on a home visit in 1965, he was in the sanitorium after falling ill while attending Churchill's funeral in bitterly cold January weather.

In a different league was the 2022 podcast *In Dark Corners*. BBC Sounds has revealed the utterly dark side, child abuse, so dangerous when it finds an entry into boarding school life. This had clearly been the case at Gordonstoun as also at other leading schools over recent decades, with the school administration resisting attempts to lay the abuse bare. Doubly shameful! 'It would be better for him that a great millstone were hung round his neck and he were cast into the sea,' as St Mark has the words of Jesus. The saying that the price of liberty is eternal vigilance is nowhere truer than in the institutional arena.

Though I never had the faintest idea of such sexual abuse, yet revisiting later over the decades I was once or twice disappointed in a lack of a sense of Gordonstoun's unique heritage. However, the current leadership, and my sense of the 'feel' of the school most recently is entirely positive. The present Principal Lisa Kerr and Chair of Governors Dr Eve Poole run a tight ship and ensure and safeguard all that is best in the precious and distinctive contribution of Gordonstoun. On a lighter note, the experience of us all at Altyre in those far away days after Philip and before Charles, as those still living gladly affirm, was happy and untroubled.

One day Mrs Chew's maid asked me in her broad Morayshire accent, 'Do you remember Andrew Stewart? Because he's coming to see you!' I had first met Andrew and Effie years earlier as a student when he was the Keeper at the remote Fealar Lodge high above Glen Tilt. Four of us had arrived out of the snowy darkness on a February night, and he had a gun in his hand when he answered the door, shouting, 'Come in, whoever you are!' They had been snowed in for six weeks and had not seen a soul since Boxing Day. We were treated royally and next morning sent off with venison sandwiches over frozen mountains to catch the skiers' bus at the Devil's Elbow. Now years later, Andrew was head shepherd at Ballachraggan on the nearby Dallas Estate. He welcomed our parties to camp on the sweet grass under the birch trees beside the Lossie, a perfect campsite for juniors, with the moorland heather above. Andrew with his smart kilt and Effie with her soft Skye accent came to be included at Altyre on various school occasions, always with the attendant hospitality of our gracious Eva and her team.

Twice, with my colleague John Gillespie, I took parties of boys to Tirol, scaling peaks and traversing glaciers as we sped from hut to hut. In 1955 we linked up in the mountains with a German family who invited me for New Year to Cologne, which had ben almost totally destroyed by the RAF. Workmen were up to their waists in the half-frozen Rhine, rebuilding the bridges. My host's pleasant home was some way from the city. As we walked down the road, he greeted an old lady who returned his *grüss Gott*. 'She is a Jewish lady who lived in our house during the war,' he said. 'When it got too dangerous, we passed her on to the next family. There were no Nazis in our street.' I thus began to learn a little about the German resistance to Hitler, which was more widespread than was commonly known in Britain.

We were expected to be back from weekend expeditions in time for Sunday evening Chapel, held in the Hall under the baleful eyes of the buffaloes, rhinos and other hunting trophies assembled on the walls above us by one of the Laird's forebears. One would sit, somewhat weary, with the mind flicking back to some river crossing or glissade earlier in the day, yet attracted to the clear truth of scripture and the clarity with which it was proclaimed in WP's Scottish voice. The Revd WP Young, MC, had succeeded Dr Hahn's intimate friend and first Chaplain, the Revd AG Fraser of Achimota.

I began to hear, often amid the laughter of those like WP who had known him, of the foibles of the founder of the school, aspects of a remarkable man. We irreverent younger staff loved the

Four staff, with Louis our Chamonix guide and his wife, 1955.

atmosphere, the provenance, the mix of inspiration and down to earth reality we experienced in that happy setting.

There is always a gap between the ideal and the real, and at Altyre it was pretty big. The school needed to grow, so was taking some boys of limited academic ability such as those with dyslexia or other then unrecognised conditions, who of course also had much to contribute. Over a pint at the Victoria in Forres there was plenty of laughter among us, whether over the boys or over our landlord the Laird. A decayed aristocracy and all the comedy of the Highlands inspired my more artistic colleagues, John Gillespie and Tony White, to a series of musical melodramas, one of which graced the Edinburgh Fringe. 'Beastie Beware' featured the Loch Ness Monster. After all, Miss MacNiven our Housekeeper who came from Drumnadrochit, had actually *seen* it! After Philip and before Charles, 'Tottering Towers' touched on our royal connections and crumbling mansion.

The Duke's Old School

Etonians are smooth as silk, and beautifully bred,
But most of them don't stay, they go to Tottering instead.
Winchester may be older, and Eton better class,
But there's one thing about Tottering that no one can surpass
For wherever you may go
Everyone will know
It's the DUKE'S OLD SCHOOL.

At Dartmouth Naval College you can study Naval Law,
But if you sail at Tottering you learn to like the shore
Winchester, &c.
If you want to go to sea,
That's the place to be –
It's the Duke's Old School

Loretto, Fettes, Rannoch – the discipline is strict,
Just the thing for savage Scots or an unprogressive Pict.
Winchester, &c.
Though they have the maddest staff,
Never, never laugh
At the Duke's Old School.

Perhaps you cannot multiply; perhaps you cannot spell:
Then you'll be quite at home – you will get on very well.
Winchester &c.
If they think that you are dumb,
Tell them that you come
From the Duke's Old School.

The surroundings are magnificent: I know that he'd adore
To sit and suck a sandwich on a sodden Scottish moor.
Winchester &c.
And it's utterly absurd
To breathe a single word
Against the Duke's Old School.

Four of us, three staff and a former teacher, Andy Clelland, were
planning to go to the Karakoram in 1957. Andy, one of the finest
post-war Cambridge climbers, had left Gordonstoun to teach at
its sister school, Anavryta in Greece, and had gone on to help
Palestinian children in the Gaza Strip, which even then was a place
of trouble and suffering. The previous years he had come to join
our staff party climbing in Chamonix and in the Dolomites. In
1956 he came again, this time to Arolla in Switzerland. On our
first day out I was unwell, so turned back. Some hours later Jo
Nold returned alone to say that a mass of rock had tipped over
on an easy ridge - they weren't roped - and Andy had been swept

46

down with it eight hundred feet. I had seen accidents before, but this was different.

My cosy life was as shattered as his body when Mr Chew and Andy's father came to Evolène for the funeral. I remember asking as a kind of prayer, 'Why did Andy die?' In an incoherent way I felt that his death should not be meaningless. I had admired his work among refugee children in the Gaza Strip, and contrasted that experience with my own easy life.

We were, however, still planning for 1957 to climb in Northern Pakistan. We had visited Tom Longstaff, aged but sprightly in retirement at Achiltibuie. He told us to go to Ishkoman, west of Gilgit. Tom had climbed Trisul in 1903 and when we asked him what he had worn at 23,000 feet he said, 'this', touching his old tweed jacket.

A colleague's uncle was the Commandant at Kakul, Pakistan's Sandhurst. He replied to my enquiry saying he could help with maps and a liaison officer, also asking if any of us would be interested in coming out for a longer period. A friend of his, Mr Flecker, wanted someone as a housemaster and to teach English at Lawrence College in the Murree Hills. I was at once interested. When friends protested that I was crazy to go to live in Pakistan, I began to make excuses, saying I would come back after seeing the world. But it was Andy's death that had started me on this new departure. Many years later I unearthed a letter from Mr Flecker. He had written that in a Muslim society the best way of working as a missionary was by one's character. So I must have asked that question.

But it was mainly with a sense of adventure that I set off on another journey, for the first time beyond the familiar culture of Britain and of Europe as it then was.

My House of fifty Boys, Lawrence College 1957.

PAKISTAN

Culture Shock and New Beginning

Woken by bagpipes each morning, served by Goan stewards and fed like kings, RMS *Caledonia* was my introduction to the East. What exceptional liners they were! Though the cabins varied from deck to deck, students, tea planters and ambassadors, British, Pakistani and Indian, mixed freely in the single class Anchor Line ships. Ten years after Partition, there was still a hint of the imperial past reflected in the graciousness of our mode of life. Fourteen days at sea allowed a leisured space between the concerns of the past and the future.

Graeme Black, a Scottish civil engineer in Rawalpindi, and I survived the Bay of Biscay's storms almost alone at the bar and relaxed in the Mediterranean sunshine. Ten miles off Port Said Graeme took me to the side and bade me smell the East. We were among the first convoys to pass through the Canal since the Suez War the previous year. The Gully Gully men, fishing live chickens from the folds of their ample garments, slipped them slyly through those of the lady passengers to the entertainment of a growing crowd, while traders, torn between patriotism and the return of business, chose the latter and sold us leather camels and prayer mats. The Canal was littered with sunken ships, but Aden was orderly and peaceful in an Indian summer of Empire. Before we parted at Karachi Graeme invited me to spend occasional weekends at his cottage in the Murree Hills, not far from my destination.

At Karachi, then capital of Pakistan, the representative of the British Council warned me that there had been 'difficulties' a thousand miles away at Lawrence College. He sent me off on the Frontier Mail. I awoke next morning to a limitless sea of floodwater, with only a thread of railway embankment rising, mile upon mile, above it. This was my introduction to a stately mode of railway travel at thirty or forty miles an hour. Leaving the flooded area, we would stop at small stations and descend from our air-conditioned seclusion to buy sweet, loose skinned oranges, *narangi*, a dozen for a few annas, while a chorus of vendors offered every kind of food. As we puffed along, respectful turbaned bearers supplied tea between excellent meals. Finally at Rawalpindi, Ronald Mackin, local officer of the British Council, met the train and entertained me in his family home with much kindness. Next day he drove me up the long succession of hairpin bends into the pine forests, up past the ruined brewery, burnt in 1947, to the Principal's bungalow at Ghora Gali. Only then did I come to know that my Irish predecessor had left in a hurry after a threat to burn down his house. Ronald's assurance that he could come and pick me up at any time was hardly reassuring.

This was the first of a succession of challenges over the following months which, in spite of much positive initial experience, completely defeated me. University, National Service and Gordonstoun had all opened doors beyond my expectations. Now that lucky star was to desert me, and I would be unable to cope. Yet this was the situation which led me to reach out for that 'thank God handhold' which every climber knows, and to find within it more than I could have imagined.

God, for all of us, is present in some way behind the scenes. I think of an earlier moment, perched high up on a hard route on Pillar Rock in Cumbria. Momentarily losing balance, that vital handhold was there! Or another time, after a friend's accident in

50

bad winter weather in the Mamores, urgently needing to cross the swollen River Nevis by night illuminated by friends' torchlight beams, when for a moment the rushing water threatened to carry me away - I just got across! Or many will remember the moment when overtaking big trucks on the motorway, a fast, oncoming vehicle was suddenly very close.

If in later life we come to be assured of a gracious saving hand we can look back and say thankfully, 'Someone was there!' Looking back, that precious element of 'youth', defying age and mischance, enables us to celebrate good things in our shared rich experience. And, if growing older we have young friends the privilege is heartwarming.

I was to be the housemaster of Peake House, one of four Senior School houses, and to teach English to the 'Cambridge' Certificate classes. Peake House with its sixty boys looked out beyond the main field, and over pine covered hills to the distant plains five thousand feet below. As my quarter was still unfurnished, I was to stay with Mr Flecker until it was ready. The Fleckers' delightful daughters were visiting them, and it was only when they left and I moved into my rooms at the end of Peake House, that reality began to strike home.

Lawrence College is the Harrow of Pakistan. It was founded in 1860 by Sir Henry Lawrence for the Anglo-Indian community, for the sons and daughters of police officers, stationmasters and the varied resident Britons. Boys and girls were segregated but managed to pass notes across the chapel, scribbled and still visible in old prayer books. A teacher training section was added. Games fields were carved out of the hillside. Staff cottages were sprinkled up and down the small lanes. The fine stone-built church in gothic style rose from the ridge at the top. It stands at six thousand feet above sea level, a thousand feet and three miles below Murree, the hill station on the old road to Kashmir from the railhead at

Rawalpindi. The College closes for three snowbound months in winter.

After Partition in 1947 all but a few of the Anglo-Indian staff had dribbled away and were replaced by Punjabi Muslims. The girls' and teacher training sections closed. By 1957 the boys were mainly sons of Army officers and landowners (zamindars). Most were Punjabi though a fair number were Pathan. The framework of an English public school remained, with fierce attachment to tradition, real or imagined. Zamindars' sons do not have the greatest respect for teachers, some of whom, admittedly, were scarcely up to the job. The prefects tended to be more powerful than the masters.

Mr Flecker CBE had first seen the school in its spectacular outer Himalayan setting while passing through Ghora Gali by *tonga*[4] in 1917 en route for Kashmir. He had been invalided from Mesopotamia, for which Bombay was the base, and Gulmarg in Kashmir a convalescent station. The school had gone down badly after 1947 and the Governors, wishing to bring in an experienced Principal, appointed him just as he was retiring from the headship of Christ's Hospital. The British Council arranged a contract, and high hopes were placed in his ability to restore standards. He told me that from his bungalow up the hill he could plan reforms and make appointments: but he needed someone to get in on the ground level. There was everything to learn in a new culture. Colleagues were friendly and I found to my surprise that being British I started on a good wicket. At least in the north-west, it appeared, British rule had been widely appreciated.

I began to plan and lead excursions into the nearby mountains. The Wali of Swat, whose nephew Aman e Room was in Peake House, invited us for half term to his mountain state

---

4   A horse-drawn cart

which was then still semi-independent. We took the College coach, pausing at the rest-house under the grim prison fortress of Attock where the blue-green River Kabul meets the swirling Indus, grey from its glacial silt. Then climbing up over the Malakand Pass we entered the lush Swat Valley and headed for the capital, Saidu Sharif. We spent the night in a splendidly constructed new college before going on up the valley to Bahrain, where we were allocated our guard, whose locally made rifle was inscribed 'Lee Enfield'. We climbed through autumn forests, sleeping in a herdsman's hut, then clambering up to a rocky summit at fourteen thousand feet where a thunderstorm caught us. Our ice axes fizzing warningly, we took the precaution of standing them in the snow and moving a few paces distant.

On our return we visited the palace overlooking Saidu Sharif where I was taken to see Aman's white-robed grandfather. He had retired, it was said, to a life of prayer and meditation. The less reverent added, 'just as well considering how many men he's finished off!' He told me that he had fought at Malakand (1898) against Sir Winston Churchill, who clearly qualified as a worthy opponent. Swat state, later absorbed as a district of Pakistan, was peaceful. We were delighted to see dispensaries, schools and the new college, all signs of the enlightened rule of the Wali and his family.

Back at school, I normally took lunch in the dining hall where the satisfying staple menu included naan or rice, dal, potato, lamb and sag or spinach, all curried in Punjabi style. Someone found me a servant, Saeed Mohammed from Punch. He was cheerful and loyal, catering to all my simple needs such as shopping in Murree, cooking, cleaning and taking messages.

At Altyre my style had been informal. One can hardly maintain formal discipline under the Shelter Stone or when cooking in a bothy. Thus I now made the mistake of being too friendly too quickly in class. Boys from other houses, making jokes across the class in Punjabi, exploited my weakness and reduced me to impotence. In the culture of the school the alternative to strong discipline was chaos, and for a long while I struggled to survive. Letters home also revealed an increasing loneliness and homesickness for the camaraderie of Altyre.

A weekend with Graeme helped, and the holidays were coming. On the last morning of term buses were due to leave early taking the boys down to the trains at Pindi. Waking in the small hours I found bonfires in progress, house furniture protruding from the flames. There were raids too, from one House to another, involving bullying. No-one else seemed worried; it was 'tradition'. I felt desolate. Could I stick it out for three years?

My long winter holiday began with a visit to Acheson or Chief's College in Lahore, the Eton to our Harrow. With its perfect lawns and Indo-Saracenic buildings it seemed a world away from Ghora Gali. Akbar's Fort, the Badshahi Mosque, Kim's Gun: there was much to see in this stunning ancient Mughal capital city.

I had arranged to explore South India with Jo Nold, now married and still teaching at Gordonstoun, so flew from Karachi to Bombay and just managed to jump on a McKinnon-Mackenzie line ship down the West Coast. We put in at Karwar and Mangalore, passing by Portuguese-ruled Goa. At Mangalore the ship stood offshore while a boat came out to take off passengers and cargo. Meanwhile we had time to wander through the pleasing lanes of tile-hung, palm shaded houses before rejoining the ship for Cochin. Jo, Andy, his wife and I hired a *wallam*, a country boat in which we travelled and lived, poling down the backwaters of Kerala. Then onward by second class train to Hyderabad, pausing to explore the impressive remains of the great fort of Golconda, ravaged by Aurangzeb. Both there and then in Delhi I stayed with ex-Gordonstoun colleagues. Gurdial Singh, with whom I had climbed

54

in Scotland, was now a housemaster at the Doon School, and later a member of the first successful Indian Everest Expedition. His family were landowners and Army Officers who treated me with the unconstrained hospitality typical of the Jat Sikh.

Returning to Pakistan I visited Hugh Tyndale Biscoe, who was teaching in Peshawar at Edwardes College. Under the shadow of the Khyber Pass the College, established by the Church Mission Society (CMS) in 1900 and even in 2022 a place of sound learning and good order, was then run by Dr Phil Edmonds. I was beginning to glimpse something of the scope of mission enterprise the length and breadth of the sub-continent. Dr Edmunds was an admirer of Kurt Hahn and quizzed me about his school. He arranged for me to stay at the Northern Scouts mess in Gilgit, the only place at that time possible for visitors. My Dakota flight from Pindi, mainly carrying sacks of wheat, scraped over the Babusar Pass at thirteen thousand feet close below the summit of Nanga Parbat, before dropping down to the little oasis of Gilgit. A Major Sher Khan took me next day up to the Air Force Ski School. He enquired about Lawrence College, adding that he and many Gilgit boys had gone to the CMS school in Srinagar, but since Partition he deeply regretted this was no longer possible.

My long holiday had been a mind-expanding escape, but the next school year was to be for me a time in the desert. Mr Flecker had been making repeated journeys to the Education Office in Lahore, where false charges had been brought against him by someone disappointed in the admission of a boy. A transparently honest man, he was caught up in a web of lies. In any event, he sadly developed polio, and left Ghora Gali on a stretcher, to die in Oxford a few weeks later. The Senior Housemaster, Mr Muin-ud-din, became Acting Principal. Muin was a good and wise man, but another housemaster began to set the boys against him. All this was par for the course and useful experience for me, though hard at the time.

Term had not long started when a message came from the office asking if I would like to put up a visiting German scoutmaster. Gladly agreeing, I was surprised to see a Long John Silver figure arriving on crutches, followed by a tail of boys. He had one leg, a patch over one eye, and wore tattered fragments of scout uniform. I had welcomed him in before realising that he was an unrepentant Nazi. He could only speak of Jews with hatred and was begging his way round the world under the pretence of being a scoutmaster. Going off to teach, I returned to find him regaling the boys with stories. Hearing that the Prefects had organised a school wide collection for him, the Acting Principal instructed me to send him off, telling him that if he accepted money the school would call the police.

As I dispatched him down through the pines, he shouted to the boys that it was because he was German and I was English. I was duly booed by the school at lunch, and later found the faithful Saeed Mohammed removing the contents of the lavatory which had been put through my letter box. Later, when things were different, I was chatting on the balcony with Jehanzeb, my Pathan Head Boy, who happened to say, 'Sir, you shouldn't have sent that German away.' 'But he was a bad man,' I said. 'I know he was, Sir, but you had taken him in as your guest,' he replied. So one went on slowly learning cultural lessons. At this stage I felt that my lucky star - though I did not believe in stars - had deserted me. Defeated by aspects of the culture, I was almost ready to run away.

The night Martial Law was declared the School Bursar - probably the man who had given false information about Mr Flecker - disappeared, and by morning was found to have departed quietly for his village. Even worse, in my innocent eyes, the staff room was full of laughter at the news. They *all knew* that he had for years been dipping his hands in the till. It was, it seemed, simply expected that anyone in such a position would make the most of it.

Perhaps because of my continued inability to deal with the humourist who trickled out Punjabi witticisms at my expense in class I became depressed. Turning from the desert within to the desert around me I tended to note only the negatives. I saw the utterly poor peasant farmers and coolies in the surrounding area, the starving *tonga* ponies with their untreated sores in Murree, women so clearly of inferior concern. Knowing nothing of Islam beyond what I had read in Fisher's *History of Europe* and without experience of the complexities of religion or of culture, I began to reflect on the confident and caring society emerging from wartime austerity in Britain. What positive and practical energising force was behind the good I had known but which seemed lacking in the strangely barren new environment? I was challenged by this very different culture and felt hopelessly lost.

Temporary relief turned up. Graeme Black's firm needed a Land Rover, and we decided that I would go home before Christmas to pick up the vehicle. Graeme would fly home later and we would drive back overland together.

If Graeme was one friend, another was Nora Glegg, the formidable but good-hearted Anglo-Indian lady who ran the Junior School. As girl and teacher she had been there fifty years in her cottage up by the church. She was the main figure in the small congregation of six or eight who read the Anglican service together on Sundays. Occasionally a visitor from Murree would lead the service, the most notable being the Revd Geoffrey Bingham, an Australian who was house father to a group of missionaries' children while he and his wife studied Urdu. He was becoming a friend when I needed one, and would introduce me to others.

Of course, there were good days. The boys in the House always wanted excursions. A memorable one started from a rest house nine thousand feet up in the forest at Changla Gali. Next morning we set off down a steep watercourse, then took a precipitous cliff path through forest and boulder beds to the Jhelum near Kohala at two thousand feet. I ended up carrying an exhausted boy to the road where a bus took us back up numerous zigzags to Murree. Another time we hired cycles to whizz down the 22 miles from Murree to Kohala before piling on a bus to return. Such excursions built up a strong spirit of togetherness. I would find relationships, birthed in shared memories of good days in mountains, so lasting that today I can call up an Old Boy, now a retired dentist living in Solihull, and we can reminisce and laugh over various days and individuals from sixty-five years past. Likewise, through all that Kashmir quarter century weekly class expeditions led us into infinitely varied mountain days remembered today. By the end of term things were past the worst, and there was much to look forward to.

I enjoyed the luxury of the Lloyd Trestino line to Genoa and Christmas at home. New Year and half of January was spent with friends in perfect winter conditions in the Cairngorms. Having collected the Land Rover, I visited a friend who said, 'You should put a winch on it.' He generally showed such awareness of practicalities that we asked Richard to join the overland party.

We set off on what became a memorable mid-winter journey, visiting my National Service contact Frans on the Semmering Pass, were arrested for camping in an ammunition depot in Turkey (it was dark, so we didn't know) then nearly buried in a snowdrift before being hauled out by a horse and tasting generous Muslim hospitality over three snowbound nights in a village house.

Entering Iran close to the Soviet border in full view of Mount Ararat, we made our way through Tabriz to Tehran, then skirted the desert southwards to Isfahan, where we camped in the grounds of the CMS Mission Hospital. On into south-eastern Iran where we were warned not to stop as there had been attacks from dacoits.

Occasional overladen trucks traversed the road, sometimes no more than a track through the wild rocky landscape. The Land Rover's rear springs suffered seriously, but in Zahedan Richard bought lengths of steel and found some Sikhs able to repair the vehicle.

Having navigated the wilds of Baluchistan we stayed with friends of Graeme in Quetta. Down through the Bolan Pass and onwards towards the Grand Trunk Road where now all seemed positively homely as we drove up through the wheat fields of the green Punjab, just in time for the new term.

In the following months something happened which was totally different from - yet a fulfilment of - anything I could have expected or hoped for when setting out for Pakistan.

I invited Geoff Bingham for dinner. He was wise enough to talk of anything but religion. Geoff had joined the Australian Army in 1941 and was made a sergeant as his unit fought their way down the Malay peninsula. He was awarded the Military Medal after leading his men to take a Japanese machine gun post, and was badly wounded. Taken prisoner, he survived the war in Changi Camp, a man in a thousand.

After a good evening I persuaded him to let me walk back with him up the steep three-mile track to Murree. A mile from the top I found that I had to help him along as his old war wound still gave him trouble. In spite of many problems he was confidently moving through life, while I was struggling. He clearly had something I desperately needed, so I laid aside my Plato and Dostoevsky and began to devour the New Testament, reading and re-reading the Gospels and the letters of St Paul. By Easter I had become sure the faith was true, about the world and about me. A personal response was clearly needed. As I went into a service in the Murree church at 3pm on Easter Sunday (the bell was just stopping ringing), using the twentieth verse from the third chapter of the book of Revelation as a prayer, I remember saying, 'I don't understand, Lord, but I'm sure it's true: please come in.' *Credo ut intelligam*, as Anselm, following Augustine, had put it. Geoff Bingham's faith was validated by a life which had faced much suffering. Though a brilliant speaker he didn't need mere words: his life spoke.

For a long time one slogs up what seems a never-ending mountain. Then the slope eases, and suddenly one is on the crest, then going easily downhill as the whole landscape opens up. With me at least it was rather like that. Several of the good things that happened over the following weeks and months could be put down to coincidence but were surely not. I had found a point of light: help in time of need in 'Jesus', who had 'come in' at this very point, and who also claims according to the account of his follower John, to be the true light that enlightens all men. Now I was to be surprised, especially in three very practical and life-changing areas. The first was transformed relationships in the school.

One morning when the usual suspects were giving me their customary treatment, I simply picked up my books and went home. Some minutes later two polite boys knocked at the door and asked when I was coming back. 'When you all decide to behave,' I replied. They went away and soon came back with some of the naughty ones. 'Sir, we'll all be good.' I returned and had no more trouble. By retreating into my room I had been putting up barriers against them. Now the barrier had fallen from my side. They were no longer 'Muslims', or 'those awful boys', but just 'my kids'. Friendship, like hostility, tends to be reciprocated. I began to enjoy their company.

Another change was highlighted when the Senior Housemaster faced a delicate problem he did not want to touch and I was asked to take charge of college discipline. I soon found out why he did not want to deal with it. A Pathan boy, bearded and bigger than me, had begun paying undue attention to a girl at the nearby convent. The girl's father, a general, added to the demands of the Mother Superior for effective action. The problem was that the boy's father was a government minister. I offered the lad a choice: expulsion or 'six of the best'. He chose the latter, which I then had to administer. For a moment I thought he was going to get up and smite me, but all went well. The matter was solved. One only has to do that once.

Over the previous eighteen months at the school, though I had enjoyed occasional weekends with Graeme Black, there was a complete desert as regards female company. Almost the only British woman I had even spoken to was Helen Qureshi, wife of a young Junior School teacher. Helen was the daughter of a Free Church of Scotland minister. Some of the Scottish mission people in the plains were concerned that she might be lonely and asked a young doctor, going up to the Murree Language School, to visit her. Helen and Yusuf, perhaps thinking I might be the lonely one, invited me along to make up the small party. Thus I found myself sitting opposite Catherine McHardy. She was beautiful. It passed belief that she had stayed in Glencoe Youth Hostel. We worked out that with a school friend, cycling across Rannoch Moor, she had been there when a crowd of students turned up, perhaps our lot. Family holidays in the Highlands revealed so many places we both knew. And right here was that person I had never quite met at St Andrews or in Morayshire.

Our courtship, carried on in that culture, provided interest to both staff and boys, also to the mission community in Murree. From the time we announced our engagement the school did its best to enrol her, co-opting her into making costumes for *Henry V* and even, Mrs Muin being unwell, drafting her in as hostess to a Pakistan Public Schools conference. Her diplomacy was severely tested by the crusty head of Karachi Grammar School, but all went well.

A newly discovered faith is contagious as it proved when a crowd of boys brought Shelby Tucker to my door. Already an inveterate hitchhiker, he looked like the earlier German mendicant. My surly 'What do you want?' was unfriendly enough to jolt him into replying, 'I came here to learn something about Christianity!' I welcomed him in, and went off to teach, leaving him my newly acquired copy of JB Philipps' *Letters to Young Churches*. He stayed for a fortnight, meeting Catherine and several impressive missionaries in Murree whose faith, like Geoff Bingham's, had been tested in wartime service. In God's providence I proved to be for him the midwife to faith in Christ, as Geoff had been for me. Our friendship continued through the decades, with Shelby, long an established author, graciously funding this publication over sixty years later.

My contract was now in its final year. I was at last happy in Pakistan and was enjoying Lawrence College. Capable teachers were in demand, and it seemed right to stay in the sub-continent. I wrote informing Mr Chew that I would not be returning to Gordonstoun.

Soon after a note arrived from Dr Edmonds in Peshawar: 'Are you thinking of being a missionary, and would you consider whether the Tyndale Biscoe School in Srinagar is not where God wants you to be?' He added that the school was likely to be taken over by the Government as the Bishop couldn't find anyone to run it. Perhaps I was the person needed? Since Mr Flecker's note, which I had totally forgotten, the thought of 'being a missionary' had never crossed my mind, but In the recesses of memory I had heard of this school, its mountain camps, its lake swims and regattas, its social service. There were echoes of Dr Hahn about it, and it felt right to us both to explore further. We decided, when the winter holidays arrived, that I would go to have a look.

Jalalpur Jattan, where Catherine was the long sought for lady doctor, is not far from the Mirpur and Kotli border of Azad Kashmir, the districts from which more than half Britain's four million Muslims originate. The hospital was part of the old Punjab Mission of the Church of Scotland. Returning from language school, she resumed work there.

To visit Kashmir, though its mountains were visible from just above Murree across a forbidden frontier, involved a six hundred mile journey via Lahore to cross that awkward frontier between Pakistan and India, then flying up from Amritsar to Srinagar, capital of the Indian state of Jammu and Kashmir.

The Tyndale Biscoe School, having survived five acting principals in the previous six years and being without one at the time I visited, looked forlorn, its crumbling fences and walls needing urgent attention. Yet meeting a few of the local staff, all Biscoe's old students, revealed a clear and astonishing family likeness to Hahn's Gordonstoun. Something of the same spirit seemed to be present in both.

It was only years later that I discovered in the person of the Revd AG Fraser the actual source of the connection. Fraser, known as Fraser of Achimota, had early been a friend of Biscoe, visiting Srinagar and greatly admiring his work of social transformation there. Many years later he became an intimate friend of Kurt Hahn in Scotland, and so impressed him that Hahn made him his first School Chaplain at Aberdovy and then at Gordonstoun.

Catherine had anyway committed herself to living in the East, and was getting to grips with an important language. I was gaining experience without which no-one should take on leadership in a different culture. The Kashmir school had links with CMS whom the Bishop of Amritsar had approached for help in filling the post. I wrote to them, and friends also wrote on our behalf. In due course CMS accepted us for long service in Kashmir.

In just a few months my life and prospects had radically changed. I was receiving remarkable training for something barely seen. There was plenty to learn and experience grew during the ensuing long winter holiday as I took up an invitation from Jehanzeb, my Pashto-speaking House Prefect, to stay at his home in North West Frontier Province. He met me off the bus at Mardan with an older relative who drove us to his home. As the car moved off, Jehanzeb said, 'He's my uncle; he's trying to kill me.' His father being dead, Jehanzeb was the landowner. The uncle, a lawyer in Mardan, had tried to persuade him to marry his daughter in order to get his hands on Jehanzeb's land. Having declined, his uncle would now be taking other means to achieve his aim.

Next morning we went out to shoot quail. The country was beautiful in its early spring colours, with fields of mustard brilliant yellow against the delicate peach blossom and the green of the emerging wheat and sugar cane, the bare Swabi hills rising to the north. My host noted every rise or declivity in the ground, saying, 'You could shoot someone from there,' and walked warily for any possibility of ambush. When I missed some quail and confessed that I wasn't much of a shot, Jahanzeb, shocked, said, 'If you're not, you don't say so!' He was not joking.

The following day we went by *tonga* towards the hills, accompanied by four retainers, their rifles pointing skyward. The track now running along the margin of cultivated land, two wild looking men leapt out of the bushes on the other side. Jehanzeb translated their plea. They were outlaws, murderers condemned to live in unadministered territory whose boundary we were on. They thought I might be an officer who could get them a pardon. We went on to an ancient hilltop fort looking out over the Vale of Peshawar. Small boys appeared out of nowhere and pressed coins into my hands, which my father later identified as belonging to the Indo-Greek period after Alexander.

I never saw Jehanzeb's mother, only a hand around the door when she brought food and when she gave me a shawl for Catherine. Jehanzeb was a very affectionate, if moody, young man. The sad sequel was that, on enquiring about him on a visit to Pakistan in 1997, forty years later, I learned that he had been hanged for murder.

I continued learning about Pathan tribal culture from boys in the House such as Masood, who had initially been brought to school carried by night across hostile tribal territory by a servant, lying hidden during daylight. When I was invited to the home in Tirah of an Afridi boy, the Deputy Commissioner in Peshawar from whom I needed a permit to pass through tribal territory, refused to give it. 'Mr Ray,' he said, 'my Afridi friend has enemies along the route you would need to travel. They might decide to take a shot at you to get even with him.'

Then on setting off for a short winter holiday with Catherine we first headed for Peshawar, staying with Dr Edmonds at Edwardes College, from where we took a bus up the Khyber Pass to Landi Kotal on the Afghan border. Declining the offer of *afeen* (morphine) in the bazaar we set off to walk. An English-speaking Pathan, seeing us move off the road to take a photograph, advised us to stay on the road. A few minutes later we again left the road by just a few steps and the same gentleman called out very abruptly, 'Get back on the road! See that trail of men over there; any of them would kill you for your camera!' Sure enough, not far distant on the hillside was a long file, maybe a hundred men, all carrying heavy loads bound for Kabul.

We then headed from Peshawar to Tank. Catherine was the only woman on the bus, and I was the only man without a rifle. She sat beside the window, having to avoid the flying spit if she stuck her head out, and as a woman, finding a problem when needing to relieve herself in that barren landscape.

We aimed to stay with friends at the CMS Zenana Mission Hospital - women only! So I was given a tent in the garden. We found the hospital guarded by soldiers, and outside the wall a male ward for gunshot wounds, in response to pressing needs. Tank was one of a chain of such hospitals set up by CMS along the Frontier over a century ago.

Over sixty years there will be changes in tribal territory. AK47s will have replaced locally made rifles. Radicalised Islam, itself in great part a reaction to grievously misplaced Western policies, has brought modern warfare to the people of the region. Yet here too Christian hospitals still give exemplary service, especially to women.

On returning Dr Theo Skinner, noted eye surgeon, greeted me warmly in spite of my poaching his precious doctor, saying he had stolen his wife from the mission too. Even today in Birmingham, long after his death, he is remembered by older Mirpuris as the doctor in the hospital 'where they make eyes'. It must have been he who was long remembered as a friend by the grandfather of Maajid Nawaz, as recounted in his book *Radical*. By such friendships are extremists brought back from the edge.

There was more to learn. Having been connected at Lawrence College with the wealthy and powerful I now met some of the poorest in the land. The Pakistani flag is predominantly green, but a white strip represents the minorities, Christian and Hindu. In the border districts with India, Christians are a minority of between two and five per cent. They are mostly the descendants of outcasts who came into the Church around 1900. Many are still landless labourers though wherever there are good Christian schools the bright ones might have a chance. Their schools and colleges have served to educate their young as well as the wider population. There has also been since 9/11 in some areas of

Pakistan a significant danger of terror attacks from radical Jamaati individuals, young Christian women being carried off and forced into marriage.

Through the hospital I met Charlie and Beatrice Chirnside, district missionaries of the Church of Scotland. Cycling along field paths with Charlie, we would be expected and welcomed, sometimes into a small church building but usually into a courtyard where the village congregation had gathered, sitting round on charpoys. There would be strong sweet tea with milk, and perhaps a boiled egg and chapatis. There would be discussion and worship in Punjabi. In one village there might be eight Christian families, in another twelve. Many of the people were thin and poorly dressed, the children with runny noses and just a cotton slip. Some would go to primary school, some not, though the Church made great efforts to see that at least the brightest went on to secondary school and to college. The preaching was homely but strong, the singing, especially of the Zaburs (Psalms), was of a quality and intensity reminiscent of Wales.

The politics of the Church were sometimes deadly; yet the faith and genuineness of many village elders was deep and real. I had only a brief glimpse of the life of people like these, though in hospital Catherine learned much more of their ways, as also of the majority Muslim community. There were no Hindus or Sikhs in the area, and Dr Skinner was unwilling to speak of the frenzy of 1947, when his Hindu friends were among the many who had perished. It was noticeable that the period was referred to, both in Pakistan and in India, as Partition rather than Independence. It still is.

Returning to Ghora Gali for a final six months I now felt very much at home in the College. Catherine came up for a second spell of language study, one of a good number of missionaries in whose worship and company I found myself, whenever I was free, warmly included. So I was also going to be one of them! Whatever the increasingly negative tone of Western discourse regarding Christian mission, the men and women I met in Murree were an impressive group. Most were in hospitals, schools or colleges, some were teaching and assisting the Church. Most of the men had seen wartime action, some in the conflict with Japan, been converted and studied theology, then returned to India to serve. All were people who could have earned good salaries in comfort yet gladly worked on a comparative pittance, often in intense heat and in primitive conditions.

One thing is clear: at whatever point in life a person begins to take Jesus as who he can be for each of us, whatever his or her religion, race or class, all past life experience will be fed into God's purposes. In my case that included everything - the good and the not so good - in the earlier part of this book.

The future beckoned, but there was some sadness in leaving Lawrence College and the Pakistan scene which had, under God, been so transformative for me. Over the following months in Britain, I was to get to know CMS until Catherine's successor arrived at the hospital, freeing her to return to Edinburgh for our wedding in the parish Church of Liberton where she had grown up.

I'm not sure when our honeymoon ended, nor perhaps if it has ever done so. We trailed our way from a highland hotel into our small tent, all round Scotland, then catching up with relations and friends old and new from the far north to Cornwall, then in Welsh youth hostels sharing with a group of young people with whom CMS had linked us. Thoughts now focused on the practicalities of the immediate future, our apprenticeships having prepared us for that land beyond the mountains, Kashmir.

PAKISTAN

School party en route for Mahadev summit, 13000ft.

KASHMIR

Shangri La and Fissured Foundations

Kashmir! Fabled Valley of dreams! The very name will have a different resonance for the poet, the historian, the politician, the soldier or the refugee.

A previous publication, *Twenty-Five Years in Kashmir*,[5] is my personal account of the immensely happy and fulfilling time from 1962 to 1986 while I was Principal of the Biscoe School in the heart of Srinagar, the place where we raised our own children, our Shangri La years. Here I include a shorter sketch of our time there and of a Kashmir that remains significant for Britain as the homeland of the majority of our four million Muslim citizens, the third generation Mirpuri Kashmiri immigrants, still often Punjabi-Pahari speakers at home.

When we went to Srinagar in 1962, 'Western' and in particular British culture was still seen by much of the world as setting an enduring, cohesive standard in a world of change. The fissures were there, but as yet unrealised. Within a decade, however, as thousands of the bedraggled hippies trailed across Turkey and Afghanistan, Islam found an added confidence in the signs of breakdown of its ancient adversary. British culture, so long envied, increasingly became derided. This has impacted, in a different way, on the attitudes of Britain's Mirpuri and wider Muslim minority.

---

5 Signal Books, Oxford 2018.

There was no thought of such developments in 1962 as we were welcomed into Sheikh Bagh. The school was an open door into the city and its people, as over the years we came to know the parents: professionals, businessmen or administrators and many more in humbler situations who managed to pay the modest fees, besides the invaluable body of school staff and servants whose children came free. We shared many of the joys and sorrows, the hopes and fears, of our neighbours, rich and poor alike. Kashmiris tend to be emotional and expressive - we felt accepted and, when the mob came down the street, the school on the road front was on occasion attacked but our house was protected. Relationships with staff and parents as well as with the boys would have been stretching enough, but there was much more.

I had known about the Biscoe School but immediately found myself manager of the Girls' School as well, where a major problem at once arose. The owners of its building in the Old City had declined to renew the lease, causing Miss Mallinson to move it to the former Chaplain's House in Sheikh Bagh just before our arrival. At our first meeting she confessed that she was leaving its care to me. There was no one else. There were no graduate teachers, no proper building and not many girls had trekked up from the city as there was now a good new Government High School. It was little more than the shell of a school. Could it survive? For the teachers who came with few pupils, relaxing under the chenar trees at Sheikh Bagh was a great improvement on the insanitary confines of Fateh Kadal. But they wanted their pay. Muriel's faithful clerk Munshi Nanda Lal presided mournfully over a fast-diminishing pile of rupees.

Action being inevitable, I regretfully terminated the services of the seven seniormost. They went with angry cries to their old schoolmate, Mrs Sadiq, wife of the Education Minister. He sent them away so they went to another, now Mrs Bakshi. She sent them to her husband, who summoned me. I was a young and inexperienced foreign head and Bakshi Ghulam Mohammed was the Head of State. Our conversation was brief. He said, 'Mr Ray, the seven sisters you have sent away are very unhappy. I advise you to take them back.' I replied in a distinctly Kashmiri manner, 'I will do as you advise, Sir. But we have no money.' He said, 'I'll give you ten thousand rupees to get started.' I next met him a few months later as Guest of Honour on Parents' Day, where he told me, in front of two thousand Kashmiris, 'Build or Bust!'

There were soon two growing schools, Biscoe and Mallinson; lower primary, junior and senior for each, occupying separate zones in a shared campus. That meant about fifteen hundred children in all in 1962, many more as a third stream made its way up the schools year by year. Our house built in 1966 looked out on what had by then become the Girls' School field with our private garden behind. The Boys' School was beyond, fronting on the busy, sometimes tumultuous, sounds of Lal Chowk. Memories of seeing brother and sister, older and younger children in little groups, crossing the field homewards after school, remain indefinably pleasing. The Hostel, built back in 1910, was home to Ladakhi boys, Buddhist, Christian and Muslim, some of whom did not return to their families throughout their entire school career, travel over the Zoji La being impossible in the long winter holiday. They were early playmates of our children, as were the few other staff children resident in the campus at Sheikh Bagh.

The school was unique in that it had been the nursery and engine for social change and for Western education in Kashmir. Its CMS missionary founders, within living memory when we arrived, had opened the way into the modern age to a degree hard to visualise today. A reading of Tyndale Biscoe's autobiography[6] will show the depth of change he pushed through, using his staff and

---

6 *Tyndale-Biscoe of Kashmir*, Seeley, Service & Co., London, 1951.

boys as the means to do so. So it was that the origin of the State
Fire Service in a largely wooden city where fires were common
and dreaded, was the school fire pump, manned by his teachers.
The School Honours Board was for lifesavers. The old Central
School overlooked the River Jhelum, the main artery of trade
and the scene of frequent drowning accidents. Boys, overcoming
their dread of Jinns, were taught to swim to become ready and
able to save life. Child marriage in a city ravaged by cholera left
child widows unable to remarry, commonly used as prostitutes in
their dead husbands' families. Biscoe tackled this by charging a
married boy double fees (to pay for his wife). Also, in a Brahmin
society ruled by tradition where the remarriage of a widow was
unthinkable, it was his master Shanker Koul who first broke the
tradition as late as 1928 by marrying one.

Early on I saw the Prime Minister, Bakshi Ghulam
Mohammed, alight from his car to salute the lady I was talking
with, Miss Mallinson. Greatly revered and loved, she said to me, 'I
didn't come to Kashmir to run a school but to be with the women
of this City when they needed help.' She had come as a young
woman and now, forty years later, was about to leave.

I took over as Principal from Eric Tyndale Biscoe at the age
of thirty-four: time perhaps, for an end to the 'adventures and
escapades of youth'? That this was not entirely so was mainly
due to the selection and training of our senior staff by Dr Phil
Edmonds. I was thus able most weeks to take a class of boys and
their teacher on a 'class expedition', exploring the countryside
into the surrounding mountains. These good adventures, shared
with teenagers who loved them, became a permanent feature
of the school and the foundation of lasting relationships. Such
immersion, I hope, kept me young until we returned to 'that far
more difficult mission field of the West', as Lesslie Newbigin called
it, in 1986 when I was fifty-eight years old.

Dr Edmonds, on coming to Kashmir as Biscoe retired in 1947, had found an extensive network of mission primary schools across the Old City with an overcrowded high school at its heart. At the spacious campus I later inherited, Sheikh Bagh, besides a small primary school, the Hadow School, later named the Tyndale Biscoe School, had just been built. There was also the Hostel for boys from Ladakh. He handed most of the other schools to their old teachers or to the State while retaining the best of the staff, all Biscoe's old students, whom he trained to a high level. These, though their welcome to us was sincere, could have largely run the day-to-day work of the school without me. All except Mr Salam ud Din, the Vice Principal, were Pandits as Kashmiri Brahmins are known. He chose four as Housemasters, able men of high standing in the local community, Muslim or Hindu. These, with Arjunath Mujoo whom he made Bursar, were all honest, wise and reliable servants of the school which was their lives' centre.

After Edmonds left in 1954 no effective replacement had been found. For some time Miss Mallinson had been in nominal charge, signing the cheques but leaving day-to-day running to the local staff. In 1960 Eric Biscoe, retiring as head of a school in New Zealand, had come back to the home of his youth to save a parlous situation until a permanent successor could be found. We therefore took over from Eric and his wife Phil. They had mended fences and demolished encroachments on Sheikh Bagh. It was by then an immensely valuable piece of real estate with greedy eyes only kept at bay by old students now in high positions, wanting to see their school flourish again. It was my job to see that it did. I could not have started on a better wicket.

While both Boys' and Girls' Schools had enormous problems, they also had bodies of old students determined to enable success. It seemed that we were accepted as part of it all.

75

Guests welcome to a Girls' School occasion.

The newly formed Joint Management Committee held its first meeting just as I was appointed. Its local members raised much of the money for us to build, with the outstanding Principal of the Government College for Women, Miss Mahmooda Ahmed, at the heart of it. From the start she was an ally, though a formidable one in part due to her being a friend of Indira Gandhi, single minded in her life work for the uplift of Kashmiri women. The school had been known simply as the CMS Mission School for Girls. The first meeting of the Management Committee, the Bishop coming up from Amritsar as Chairman, considered whether its name should continue. I hesitantly asked if we should move away from a name suggesting western dependence. Mahmooda scornfully said, 'Only one name is *possible* for this school.' The matter was closed.

As well as the seven sisters, now back with few girls to teach, Muriel had employed one or two younger ladies, but we urgently needed a Head. In response to advertisement through the wider Church Miss Mavis Demta from distant Bihar was found. A sincere Christian and a mature teacher, she proved equal to the testing situation, acceptable to teachers and parents, never fazed by crisis, steady and loyal.

Things began to improve, numbers to grow, a sizable classroom block coming up and the wider community assured that the school had a future. Mavis was not there for the long term, and a tremendous breakthrough came when Miss Premi Gergan, of a distinguished local Christian family, offered to give up her lectureship in a leading Calcutta college and come for the long term.

She was my closest colleague, a delightful person of deep faith and strong character. From the beginning her leadership was purposeful and dignified, and within a few years our friends at the Presentation Convent across the river had a Christian school of some distinction to vie with. The Convent insisted on English spoken at school. Premi's was also an English medium school, but welcomed Kashmiri or Urdu outside the classroom.

The four Senior School houses in the Boys' School were named after four Kashmir mountains: Kolahoi, Haramukh, Tatakuti and Mahadev. The nearest, Mahadev at thirteen thousand feet, was climbed annually in the first weekend of June by the 10th Class of about a hundred and twenty boys on a three-day expedition. The others, higher and more formidable peaks above the Valley, were sterner tests. Each was climbed by one or more parties in my time. When the highest, Kolahoi at nearly 18,000 feet, was climbed in 1968, two girls were in the party led by two enthusiastic officers from the High Altitude Warfare School, the Girls' School by then sharing in some of our activities. In what other school would twelve-year-olds swim three and a half miles across the lake, climb high mountains and enjoy exciting weekly inter-house *shikara*[7] races and annual camps, with 'advance camp', a base for further exploration, at about twelve thousand feet? The annual Dal Cross day in July was a highlight, when most years over a hundred

---

7 Based on a traditional Kashmiri wooden paddle boat.

boys swam across the lake and about twenty swam back, the seven-mile 're-cross'. All staff shared in the leadership and organisation needed to follow such a programme safely. We never lost a boy.

A critic suggested that I ran the school like an Outward Bound school. That was an exaggeration. We would have speedily lost the support of our middle-class parents as well as the favour of the State Government had we not consistently been at or near the top of the annual 'results' table of the Matriculation examination, with a good proportion of the students attaining medical or engineering courses. This again was due to Dr Edmonds' selection and training. Each of the housemasters was also head of a department. Mr Balji Saproo for Maths, Mr Sat Lal for Science, Mr Kashinath Dhar for English and Mr Amarnath Mattoo for Social Sciences. We enjoyed the strong, sometimes enthusiastic, support of parents like those who turned up at Nehru Park to help the last weary 're-crossers' climb out of the Dal Lake after seven or eight hours in the water, or the few who came by car for the campfire and impromptu 'dramas' under the stars on the last night of camp at some faraway place in the Pir Panjal.

To counter the divisive aspects of religion Biscoe had begun mixing boys, Hindu and Muslim. The crew of a *shikara* or the makeup of a small party always had both. In later life Ravi or Arshad would be remembered, not as a 'proud Pandit' or an 'ignorant Muslim', but as a good crew member. A small group finding its way through the mountains makes for a bond of friendship; countless such memories form friendships that endure.

By 1962 Kashmir was developing fast, but unsurprisingly, as Central Government poured in money, corruption increased. Following Sheikh Sahib's removal and imprisonment at the behest of the Congress right wing, his lieutenant, our old student Bakshi Ghulam Mohammed, continued much of his beneficial policy. Personally popular, too much money leaked out at the seams, such that on our arrival we were greeted with the surprising news that Kashmir was ruled by the BBC. This was promptly explained as the 'Bakshi Brothers Corporation'. Kashmir was becoming notorious across India for corruption.

In this setting the school was prized for its discipline and smartness, and in this society where corruption ran very deep, for its peculiar addiction to truth and honesty. As such, we did not keep two sets of books but paid staff what was in the book. We actually prevented cheating in examinations. Our friend Father John Macmahon, Principal of our rival establishment Burnhall, was appointed Examination Superintendent for the Matriculation Centre for city schools set up in our school hall. On one occasion a candidate left, slipping out through a window. The paper was not to his liking, so he thought it best to produce a convincing sick note, ten rupees at most, and not fail the paper. Father Macmahon, who had duly checked him in, was surrounded by his friends who said in chorus, 'He was not here, Sir. We are witnesses!' As he later said to us, 'false witnesses.' In this setting our valued friends included civil servants and professionals, often our old students, who sought to resist and minimise or prevent corruption.

A corrupt system is hard to clean up. This was most difficult for those wired into it by family ties. We knew of a young man much influenced by Father Borst in the Baramulla school, who resisted the invitation to sit down with other electricity meter readers at the end of the day to share out the loot and pass the expected sum up the line. Losing his job, he was then beaten by his father who had doubtless paid good money for his appointment. On one occasion when we simply gave the amount shown on the meter the electricity went off and the Assistant Engineer took a very long time to re-connect us. Or a forest guard would charge a set rate for illicitly permitting a forest contractor to cut a tree or a poor family to take brushwood. But the guard was paid so little that he could hardly feed his children. So everyone gained. Only the forest became *gharib*, impoverished.

Mr Kashinath, Haramukh Housemaster, was cycling out to Regatta with me one Wednesday when I said to him, 'Everyone here takes and gives bribes. Are our Old Boys just the same?' Hesitantly he replied, 'Yes, they do too - but they know it's wrong.' I later retailed this to Dick Lucas, long the minister of St Helens, Bishopsgate. 'Ah yes,' he said, then after a pause, 'the Old Testament before the New.'

Among chief ministers of the State, one I knew and liked well was Mr GM Sadiq, a deeply honest man. Even his son Rafiq's wedding was an unfashionably modest affair. In a Moral Science class I said at one point, 'Thanks to Sadiq Sahib we have a health service and free schools for everyone in Kashmir; but the rats are eating the flesh off the bones by corruption.'[8] A lad spoke up: 'Sir, if our fathers didn't make a little extra we couldn't come to this school!' Perhaps none of us had clean hands.

It can be dangerous to challenge corruption. On our Roll of Honour Chimed Gergan, Game Warden, is recorded as giving his life for the purity of the public service in Kashmir, He had brought a smuggler to trial who, released by a corrupt judge, shot Chimed when he tried to apprehend him again the following year. Biscoe sought some justice and Chimed's brother Skyabilden was given the post. Mr Gergan, Premi's father and the head of his Ladakhi Christian family, was a friend in Srinagar who became our elder daughter's godfather.

It was, of course, the poor who suffered most. Returning from leave in the UK by ship in 1965 I received a cable, handed to me on a plate by a steward at dinner. It read, 'School burned

---

8 I continued the practice of reading from the Bible daily at Assembly, but also inherited an excellent series devised by Catholics, which was essentially Christian ethics.

down. Return immediately.' But we were sailing down the Red
Sea! Fortunately, the captain was able to arrange a flight from
Aden, so I was back quickly, leaving the family to follow at leisure.
The Senior School main classroom building on the roadside had
mysteriously caught fire at night. Not a day had been lost, with
classes using the Hostel, even storerooms and a garage. Mr Salam
ud Din said, 'Your first job is to get the servants out of the *thana*.[9]
They were all there on damp straw, and very glad when I asked
the officer in charge to let them out. It was normal to question the
servants first, and use minor torture in doing so. Each man had a
cigarette burn mark behind his ears.

Corruption, double talk and abuse aside, one learned to
appreciate the positives, the goodwill one met daily; the gifts of
artistry, humour, hospitality and much more.

To understand why Kashmiris were known across India for
their corruption and deceit one only needed to look to their history
of immense cruelty. From medieval times the rich and fertile
Valley had been the prey of outsiders: Moghul from Agra or Delhi,
Afghan, Sikh from Lahore and Dogra from Jammu. Their Afghan
and Sikh governors would loot for their masters and then for
themselves. The Old City doorways were built extraordinarily low
to impede the Afghans who would enter on horseback and carry
off the women. In their time, and earlier under Aurangzeb, Hindus
had been cast into the river if they did not become Muslims. Many,
such as the Nehru family, migrated to India. Then under the Sikhs
those who had become Muslim under pressure suffered in turn.

For the country people the scene was different but no better,
great numbers of the Muslim peasantry being virtually enslaved
for *beggar* (hard labour). Many died building the mountain road to
Gilgit.

---

9 Police lockup.

Improvement began under the Dogra Maharajah Pratap Singh, urged on by British officers such as Sir Walter Lawence whose book *The Kashmir Land Settlement* has been recently republished in Srinagar, a significant recognition today of the importance of his work for the Muslim people. The early Dogra maharajahs were determined to keep foreigners out of Kashmir, and even through our time, and until revoked by Modi in 2019, a relic of this policy remained in article 370 of the Indian constitution which barred non-Kashmiri subjects from holding immovable property in the State.

In 1865 Dr Emslie, a CMS medical missionary, was asked to treat the Maharajah and became the first foreigner to be allowed to winter in Kashmir. Permission, only granted thirteen years later, came too late for him as he died after exposure in a blizzard on crossing the Pir Panjal, having stayed too late in the year in the Valley. Thereafter the medical mission and school became cautiously accepted and then increasingly in demand as Kashmir slowly emerged into the modern world.

Centuries of tyranny had left society in the social and moral morass that Biscoe found in 1890, the basis of his lifelong determination 'to make jellyfish into men'. A casual reading of his autobiography grates in today's democratic age. It reveals the pre-1947 imperial scene. Biscoe's relatives included an admiral and a general. He was a controversial figure in the evangelical missionary setting, his nose twice broken in boxing at school, converted under Moody at Cambridge, and making use of all the privileges of his age and connections to support his fifty-seven-year determination to change society in Srinagar, to clean up the filth and reform all aspects of life. He did this with humour and his memory was loved and revered by Kashmiris, Brahmin or Muslim. While in Britain on furlough in 1922 he said that he was doing all he could for the boys, but someone was needed for the girls. Muriel Mallinson responded with her life of loving service.

It was in such a privileged situation of influence that I found myself in 1962. Any new headmaster will think carefully before changing the practice he inherits. I was able to reap the benefits of all that Dr Edmonds had already built on the basis of Biscoe's wonderful life and work. There was little, as I saw matters initially, that wanted change. The one significant addition I made to the already amazing range of activities was to introduce weekly class expeditions which replicated what I had introduced in Scotland.

To lead parties off the beaten track one needed maps, but to be seen with a map would at once bring suspicion. As the last of the old brigade, Miss Mallinson, had passed on to me a complete set of the marvellous 'half inch' sheets of Kashmir. Every footpath, mountain stream and settlement had been accurately recorded in the Survey of India more than a century earlier, the Sikh surveyors and their equipment carried by mules far from any road. The maps I kept in a cupboard after making necessary sketch notes.

In the Kashmir setting with the bus station opposite the school, early each Friday morning with thirty children and their class teacher I would pile into the back of a country bus to any of the beautiful side valleys unknown to tourists, climb through the forest to some ridge or viewpoint looking to high mountains, or reach a distant lake. Typically continuing down to a shaded stream, the party would open their tiffin carriers to eat and rest before walking on to some rural terminus of another bus, and so home. We would also visit remains of an ancient temple, a palace or canal system reminding us of the reality of a rich kingdom centred on Srinagar twelve centuries ago.

This weekly routine could be a problem for the teacher responsible for timetabling. In our case Mr Balji, among his many duties, patiently coped with whatever problems I gave him, just as the second master at Gordonstoun had done in Scotland. Both enjoyed the camps and climbs, so tolerated my complicating their duties.

Apart from the school there was more. Agreeing to be the 'Unofficial Representative' for Kashmir to the British High Commission in New Delhi meant that those who met difficulty or misfortune would come to us for help. When there was war in 1965 and 1971, I arranged a bus for those wanting to leave, though in fact no-one did. Anyone in trouble would find their way in need, or often simply a visitor asking for a little advice. A knock on the door could herald anything from tragedy after an accident to a hippy on the Zoji La, a Government minister, a police officer or a would-be parent vainly waving high denomination notes. We never knew who would be next to welcome in at the door, or to direct elsewhere.

The small Christian community was centred for us on All Saints Church a mile up the river, and on Holy Family Church for our Roman Catholic friends the Mill Hill Brothers and the Sisters of the Presentation Convent.

The Revd Yonathan Paljor, just my age, was the faithful pastor of All Saints from before 1970 until long after we had left. Born in the Moravian congregation in Ladakh, he not only led the Church but was seen by all as the representative of the community in times of stress such as the two fires, in both of which he and his family lost everything. There was a core local membership and a great variety of non-State subjects from all parts of India and beyond: civil servants and military, students from Nagaland and Mizoram, our non-Kashmiri teachers, and tourists both Indian and worldwide.

Our congregation sometimes included a senior Army officer who was able to get a truck enabling us to visit every Christian home, some thirty or so in scattered, mostly rented homes around the city. Singing well-loved carols, we were then invited in - an abiding memory. Yonathan's place was taken on his retirement by Pastor Vinoo Kaul, our old boy and son of Chandra Pandit, a Kashmiri Pandit convert and for a long time the Hostel Warden. On the fringe of All Saints, but especially welcome in our home, were three who had come out of their own Kashmiri Muslim culture and faith, whose lives I enlarge upon. To me they were the fathers of the Kashmiri Church. God had lifted them out of their Muslim faith with little or no involvement by foreign or Western agency.

In All Saints I found myself a lay reader. Pastor Yonathan spoke Western Tibetan (Ladakhi) and Urdu, but initially limited English. A church in a State capital needed English as well as Urdu services for its India-wide, indeed worldwide congregation. Bishop Nasir said I could help more if he ordained me. At a second request by his successor I felt it was right to accept, and so was duly ordained Presbyter of the newly founded Church of North India. The centre of our calling remained the schools where, though a doctor, Catherine for five years ran and greatly improved the Girls' Primary School. She had earlier taught our three children through the primary years, using the PNEU[10] materials. All her gifts were fully stretched week by week.

It may be asked in what sense we were Christian schools. I think in that context it was in what we did, and - even more - what we aimed to do in terms of character. Nearly all the children, and most of the staff were Muslim or Hindu. Whether from practice or policy we normally sought Christians as heads of the separate Lower Primary, Junior and Senior departments, and for the Hostel. The Bible was used in assemblies. This was acceptable, both locally and in the wider sphere of India, which has long treated 'minority institutions' generously in this regard. Equally important, the practice in all those years remained unchallenged locally. I tended to read stories from the gospels or narrative passages from the Old Testament, such as David in the wilderness, avoiding doctrinal passages in the epistles and elsewhere.

---

10 now Worldwide Education Trust.

We were not the sole mission or overseas personnel in the schools who gave costly and notable service. Kashmiri Christians with the qualifications and experience to take leading roles included Savitri Kaul, the daughter of a Christian Kashmiri of Pandit background and Rajinder Kaul, of similar heritage. These were both old students and State Subjects, as was my eventual replacement, Parwez Kaul.

I was obviously the last overseas Principal, and the Diocese was always looking for a Christian fit to take over. This was a sensitive matter with loyal local staff, one or two poor appointments having been made. One who had been sacked from his post as Director of a radio station by Indira Gandhi when she declared her 'Emergency' was recommended to me by the Bishop. He took over as Bursar, sorted out some difficult problems and people, then decided to sort me out and take over the school. CMS in London was rather impressed, but Bishop Aziz was not, and sacked him.

Further overseas input came from a long succession of 'gap year' volunteers in both schools. They related well to older children and junior staff, teaching English, helping with games and activities, often simply doing whatever they did best, and were valued as cultural bridge builders within the school community.

Those who want a broader picture of Kashmir will find it in Victoria Schofield's *Kashmir in Conflict*,[11] a sympathetic and authoritative history. Wajahat Habibullah was Kashmir's senior civil servant in terrible times and subtitles his *My Kashmir* (Penguin, 2014) 'The Dying of the Hope'. A longer perspective is that of another friend, the late Dr Mohammad Ishaq Khan in his *History of Srinagar 1846 to 1947*, published there in 1978. I prize the copy he gave me.

---

11 5th edition, I.B. Tauris, London, 2021.

To have a deeper understanding of Kashmir and of Kashmiris is important in view of the large number of Mirpuri Kashmiris in Britain, our largest ethnic minority, and especially because of their concentration in small ethno-religious enclaves. Mirpuri Pahari is the most widely spoken vernacular in this country. They have never spoken the Kashmiri language and only had a remote relationship with the history and culture of the Valley, but the cry of Muslim brotherhood can be a factor in British political life and has proved open to abuse by international radical forces, especially as a response to white racism and ill-thought-out policies. Today such voices have less traction, as in the third or fourth generation more mature British Mirpuri practice increasingly turns to succeeding in the British context.

Earlier this year I had a letter from Mohinder, now in his fifties and living in British Columbia, who matriculated from the Tyndale Biscoe School in 1985. He writes of his extraordinary happiness at recalling 'the best years of his life', calling his time there his Shangri La days. And they were Shangri La times too for the people of Kashmir. Between the poverty and obscurantism of the past and the tragedies since 1990, including the forced migration of almost the entire Hindu community, they were an interlude of comparatively peaceful progress for very many Kashmiris as well as a time of newly acquired wealth. But Shangri La also suggests unreality, a mirage. During those good years the seeds of future trouble were not, perhaps could not be, fully addressed.

And Shangri La was rooted in the memory of a place and an age when, especially in the villages, an immemorial scene appeared set in stone. The shepherd still grazed his flock on the leaves of the willow under which he sheltered, looking to the mountains beyond the stream, and even the city dweller warmed himself with a charcoal *kangri*[12] under his capacious *pheron*.[13] Few in the 1960s thought of climate change and the torrent of 'development' had barely begun. The unearthly beauty of the landscape remained. Even the social scene, a delicate balance between Muslim and Kashmiri Pandit, appeared durable. At least in appearance, Shangri La was there, behind the majestic Pir Panjal mountains. In the words of the Sufi poet, 'If there is paradise on earth, it is here! It is here!'[14]. But, both politically and otherwise it was a Shangri La built on fissured foundations. That scene is now gone, like much else, banished to the far corners.

They were optimistic times for Kashmir. The wars with Pakistan in 1965 and 1979 scarcely touched the State, and Sheikh Abdullah's 'land to the tillers' had given Kashmiris an unknown level of prosperity. For the lowest paid work, immigrant labour from poorer areas like Rajasthan or Bihar was brought in. The capital city of over a million souls was bustling and confident.

Kashmir is, however, one of the world's continuing areas of tension. At the junction of cultures, religions and powers, three of them nuclear, it could scarcely be otherwise. The growth of radical religion, combined with an unstable political situation and manipulation by outside powers, has since the 1980s brought its people great suffering. Under the Modi regime political opposition is silenced, and the cry of *Azadi!* has little room for expression. Kashmiris will make money and laugh at rulers who know nothing of their language, their wit and their gifts of irony and sarcasm.

For those not aware of the history it may be worth filling in a fuller outline, as this is relevant to what follows in the next chapter. About two-thirds of the British Indian Empire was ruled directly from London, the remainder being the preserve of the 'native

---

12 A clay fire pot in a wicker basket.
13 A loose baggy sleeved over garment from neck to calves.
14 Amir Khusro, 'Couplet 7'.

states'. In Kashmir, the largest of these, while the British remained the supreme power, the Dogra Maharajah ruled, or misruled. Siding with the British against his Sikh overlord in 1846, Gulab Singh had paid Britain 'seventy-five lakhs of rupees' for this vast area. A British Resident in Srinagar kept watch over foreign policy as concerns grew at Russian expansion on the northern border of the State by the 1880s. The Resident also used his influence to improve the conditions of the Muslim majority in the Valley, who in the nineteenth century were little more than slaves.

In 1931 Sheikh Abdullah came to the fore as the leader of protest, and, whether in prison or in power till his death in 1983, was well named Lion of Kashmir. As independence loomed, the British had advised the rulers of the native states to accede to Pakistan or India depending on their geographical position and the religion of their people. Maharaja Hari Singh's Kashmir adjoined both. His people were overall majority Muslim but with a Hindu majority in Jammu and Buddhist in Ladakh. He temporised perhaps hoping to be independent, but as Pathan tribesmen swept into the Valley two months after Independence, he asked Nehru to fly in troops, acceded to India and fled to Bombay. He had let Sheikh Abdullah out of prison in time for him to rally the militia and become Prime Minister as India and Pakistan went to war. Sheikh Abdullah's vision was for all Kashmiris, Hindu as well as Muslim, and it was he, in 1947, a longtime friend of Pandit Nehru, who facilitated the Indian takeover. He was in turn thrown out of power and into prison seven years later at the bidding of the Congress right wing.

Kashmir was saved from the mass killing that afflicted the Punjab, East and West, which even today 1947 is remembered not as independence but as Partition. The 1949 United Nations-brokered ceasefire included provision for a referendum, but endless negotiations were never finally clarified as to whether the question was 'India or Pakistan' or the three-way question adding the choice of independence. No referendum was ever held. It is very clear seventy-five years later that the 1949 ceasefire line will remain the boundary for the foreseeable future.

India's section, the State of Jammu and Kashmir, includes Ladakh with a Buddhist majority and Jammu with Hindus, both provinces having large Muslim minorities. Kashmir province is now almost entirely Muslim, the Hindu (Pandit) minority having fled in the course of the violence of 1990.

The area ruled by Pakistan, about a third of the total, includes the Northern Areas centred on Gilgit and 'Azad' or free Kashmir (called POK, Pakistan Occupied Kashmir, by India) which consists of most of the area west of the Pir Panjal mountains of the former Jammu Province. The majority of all Britain's Muslim population today are descended from one small area, mainly Mirpur District, of this region.

Mirpuri Punjabi, spoken at home by over a million British people even today, is 'hill people's language', and is not given the esteem of Urdu and is deserving of more status. Mirpuri people, sturdy hill farmers, came in large numbers to Britain when their land was flooded for a World Bank scheme in 1958. It may be true to comment that their cohesion as a minority community has been strengthened by consolidating in what Philip Lewis calls ethno-religious enclaves, but the negative of this is the perpetuation of entrenched patriarchal society, especially in the treatment of women by community elders with no care for today's advances. This was highlighted by Dame Louise Casey in her 2016 review into Opportunity and Integration. The education of women and the slow moving out into mixed areas in turn challenges such conservatism and helps a wider degree of integration.

New Mirpur is now one of the wealthiest cities in Pakistan, full of the second homes of British nationals living in cities such as

Birmingham. Mirpuris in Britain, many of them now flourishing, often call themselves Kashmiris. though they speak no Kashmiri, the language of the Valley. Older Birmingham friends grew up trilingual, with Pahari, Urdu and English. Inter-continental first cousin marriage has only very slowly declined.

We had arrived in Srinagar recently married in January 1962 after a two-day bus journey through the mountains, to an enthusiastic welcome on all sides. The two schools founded in British times had been a, perhaps *the*, source of enlightenment for a hitherto oppressed people. Though Biscoe's school had initially benefited the Hindus most because the *maulvis*[15] had told Muslims not to attend as they would be converted, Sheikh Abdullah saw how central the CMS work had been for the uplift of the Kashmiri people as a whole, regardless of religion. Not surprisingly, five of the six Chief Ministers of the State and most of their wives and children during our period were Old Boys and alumnae.

Every one of our Kashmir years was full of surprises: a flood, a fire, a riot or a war, yet none of this affected the satisfaction of working together in a school such as ours or of acceptance in a society and culture which at that period appeared so full of hope. That its foundations were fissured was not apparent to me in the 1960s and 1970s. It was the Iranian revolution of 1980, though Shiite, that was the signal for a raised Islamic awareness. In Kashmir, fuelled by Pakistani and Afghan 'mujahidin' influence, this increasingly included training and weapons and led to the weakening, perhaps the end, of the long tradition of *Kashmiriyat*, of a living together, even a common use of shrines among Muslim and Hindu, which had long marked the tolerant peacefulness of Kashmir. We had noted that the sons of several of our Pandit staff tended to find work and settle in Jammu, Delhi or Bombay. From about 1980 one

---

15 Religious scholars.

could not remain unaware of the heightened religious fervour and the increased lure of Pakistani-based radicalism.

It was three years after we returned to England that radical muezzins, not local Kashmiris, began their chilling nightly calls on the mosque loudspeakers for all Hindus to leave - or die. Almost that entire unique and tenacious community, including some of our best teachers, left after a few murders in the following months. We returned for a first visit nineteen years after we had left, in 2005, to find the fever had passed. It was then, in conversation with a bright village lad, that I commented on a hopeful new spirit in the Valley. 'It's a renaissance!' was his jubilant reply. On a second visit in 2012, meeting Sheikh Abdullah's grandson Umar Abdullah, the then Kashmir Chief Minister, a hopeful spirit remained strong.

Alas it has not survived the return of further political breakdown, repression and a new more widespread religious nationalism in Modi's India. Hope for freedom, *azadi*, for Kashmiris is for the time being silenced. They will take refuge in humour and, as often in history, keeping their thoughts to themselves among a senior officialdom of outsiders who know nothing of the Kashmiri language or culture.

KASHMIR

Church, people and food: St Christopher's.

FROM KASHMIR TO BIRMINGHAM

St Christopher's and the Springfield Project

Returning to Kashmir after UK leave in 1968, I needed to see our school lawyer on some small matter. Mr Shambu Nath Dhar, an Old Boy of the school, with his RAF moustache and smart blazer, was the epitome of the Hindu Englishman. Deeply troubled, he greeted me, asking, 'Mr Ray, what *has* happened to England?' 'Plenty,' I said. 'Why do you ask?' Pausing at every phrase, he replied, 'I saw an Englishman... without shoes!... begging!... in a temple!' His shock was deep. A cornerstone of his world had collapsed.

It was Indian and Kashmiri friends returning to their own country after time in the UK who first spoke to me of Western cultural collapse. Were our foundations, like Kashmir's, also deeply fissured? Our Senior Teacher, Mr Sat Lal, said to me on his return to Srinagar after a term at Gordonstoun in 1969, 'You people have thrown it all away!' This understanding steadily increased, feeding into a sense of my own country as the place where 'mission' was most needed though it was very unclear of what it should involve. Visits to the UK and the longer visits to us in Kashmir by gap year students confirmed the sense of a social revolution.

Until the 1960s the British had been respected though not loved. They still set the standard for independent India, with the Indian Civil Service held up as a continuing model of probity. Its middle-class men had adopted much of the good practice and even initially the dress of those who had set the standard for their newly independent country.

Whether the search was for Eastern spirituality, or cheap hashish, or both, something important in the West had finally cracked as the Beatles sang, 'all you need is love.' They came, these children of wealthy professionals, from California, from Germany, from England, staying in the cheap houseboats at the back of the Dal Lake, the children mocking and throwing stones at them. As Kashmir froze in winter they moved to Goa, and the word was, 'go to Goa to see the naked hippies.' Spilled out by the Paris student riots of 1968, as they trailed across Turkey, Iran and Afghanistan, the West, for long grudgingly admired, became increasingly disparaged and despised across the Muslim world. It was good for one thing only: making money.

It was at this time that we began to feel a pull to the fast-changing melting-pot of our own country. But the reasons why this change, amounting to the sudden very visible collapse of the culture that all the world envied, had happened as and when it did could only be appreciated more fully when we went to live in Sparkhill nearly twenty years later.

None of us see the whole picture. Westerners brought up within strict boundaries such as some traditional Catholic or Brethren households, or equally those with tightly limited social or economic horizons saw it as a time of apparently boundless new freedoms.

Before most observers, Lesslie Newbigin had grasped what he termed 'the cultural captivity of Western Christianity as a challenge to a missionary church'. Newbigin was initially a lone figure, warning that the new century would see a major confrontation between the materialist West and renascent and angry Islam, where the churches were too often sleeping, caught up in intellectual arguments, or simply lacking the fire of the Gospel.

All this chimed with what we were beginning to understand as we too saw the decay, even the depravity, stealing in over the following years. I began to realise that what Dr Meissner had perceived at Salem and Gordonstoun as an historian, Bishop Lesslie had, like him right back in the 1930s, understood as a theologian and a pastor. It included both the breakdown of culture and the loss of even a nominal adherence to religion and its teaching. Wherever the post-Enlightenment church of the West had been obsessed by an intellectual battle with secularism, it had lost its spiritual power and failed both in its Gospel message and in loving care.

We had followed Lesslie Newbigin's books written in India, starting with *Honest Religion for Secular Man* in 1964 when he was Bishop in Madras. It was in South India that he developed his clear understanding; that it is in our day-to-day meetings that we have real connection across faiths with fellow human beings; maybe drawing water from the well or travelling by local bus. He found little meaningful interaction in talking about religion. In Birmingham, too, practical 'dialogue' is importantly about being a good neighbour, eating curry together, family coming and going; it is about slowly deepening friendship, something precious that should not have an ulterior intention beyond prayer. God's spirit creates dissatisfaction and a desire for something better. In the British situation of freedom many Muslim people, to come to a point of questioning fundamentals, simply need continued exposure through contact with genuine Christians over a long period. Sometimes they do not need that. God speaks to them directly. I think of one Birmingham friend who, after a period of disillusionment with Islam and a search through Judaism and Buddhism, telephoned the (fortunately) female curate of St John's in Sparkhill. She said to her, 'If you're searching on the net, don't look for Christianity; look for Jesus.' She looked and found.

It was in Birmingham that Newbigin met the strong assertion of Islam in the face of a godless society. In his seventies and eighties, he modelled a loving whole life engagement with his humble practical witness in the inner-city setting of Winson Green. He combined a deep respect for Muslims on account of their faith commitment as the basis for action in public affairs, while also believing Islam to be profoundly wrong in its divergence from the Christian story.

The funeral in 2017 of Annie Rahi, the wife of his Punjabi evangelist, was held in his church in Winson Green. There I found myself in the midst of the congregation he had done so much to build towards his ideal that the 'colour coding' of the Church should reflect that of the area. It was a visible foretaste of the multicultural City of God.

We are among the many unknown figures who have also returned to urban Britain after long absence to find it changed in strange and, in some matters, unwelcome ways. We returned, not to the England I had earlier known, but to inner-city Birmingham as it was in the 1980s.

One learns a lot and can contribute something by being a trustee of a charity. But one is likely to learn much more by being a volunteer, getting one's hands dirty, or in this case sitting on the floor.

It was on home leave in 1984 that a friend had said of Sparkbrook in Birmingham, 'This is the place for you!' But how? In education, in the church, in the community? Two years later St John's, Sparkhill, sold some property and advertised for 'a church worker to reach out to the Asian community and help the church do the same.' As I was ordained in India I could not, in C of E terms, be a church worker, and so found myself a curate. There were about twenty elderly white worshippers at the front, and a similar number of black ones, mainly from St Kitts, at the back of a spacious and beautiful 1890s building. Thus began a God-given twenty-seven years, longer than in Kashmir, in England's second city.

We had joined St Christopher's in 1995, having bought a house nearby on my retirement. One Sunday in 1998 the then vicar said, 'If the Holy Spirit has really been among us, we should be doing more about loving our neighbours.'

Our neighbours were mainly British Pakistani Muslims. The church was getting to know some of them through the large mums and toddlers group, led by two members who were also primary school teachers, which had uncovered great need in the community, by then mainly composed of second or third generation Mirpuri Pakistanis. Though some were flourishing, many were poor, and given that first cousin intercontinental marriage was still running at over 50 per cent in that community, and therefore the home language was Punjabi-Pahari, there were large numbers of mothers who had little English and were very isolated. Children at school entry were twelve months behind the average, and it wasn't intelligence that held them back.

The vicar's announcement was the signal for a core group to get to work, and when the following year the Springfield Project was launched the church thought it was ready: certainly enough of its members were ready to explore, and there had been much heart searching and prayer. We were a church on the edge of Sparkhill, on the evangelical and charismatic side of the C of E spectrum. Socially we were a mixture. About half the members lived in the parish or very close by, including a brother and sister who had been involved since Sunday School childhood, and others who are real Brummies. There was - and is thirty years later - a sprinkling of professional and business folk. A friend describes us as 'a bit rough and ready, not a church of shiny Christians'.

We were blessed by some outstanding black members. I think of one Caribbean family, the mother a deeply spiritual matriarch, and her three daughters who have all become senior social workers and remain at the core of the church today. There were several in the church who had served long periods overseas and had language skills, and there were just two from 'other faith' - Hindu and Sikh - families. There were those who could love and nurture them. Many had seen the area 'go Asian' and many prayed for it, focusing on the group of ladies who had volunteered in the 'Seedlings' stay and play group for many years. It had doubled to forty children two mornings a week in the old church hall because so many wanted it. There was no good nursery nearby, and a great need for one.

Then and now we were something over a hundred adults in church most Sundays, and a similar number of children and young people. Our address book has many more names of folk, like Catherine and me, who are listed as 'friends living away'. It remains the heart's home for many who have had to move away. It is a place of acceptance, or rather enjoyment, of difference, of understanding and of love.

God was, and is, at work, and has persisted in bringing the right people in leadership at the right time. As vicars, we have had, first Dr Toby Howarth and Henriette, and then Tom and Jo Thomas.

The setting was unique, just where the mass of terraced pre-1914 Sparkhill housing gave way to the more open and varied mix into Hall Green, Tyseley or Moseley. Springfield primary school, across the road from the Hall, was already mainly Asian, and Woodlands Road Mosque, opposite the Church, was wholly so.

The 'launching' of the Project marked the start of a torrent of activity which within ten years saw it become a fast-growing charity, in a splendid new building on the site of the old church hall. It remained and is today closely intertwined with the church, and within six years widely seen as a model of cross-cultural working for the common good. It attracted interest from bodies as distinct as Tearfund, to whom we became a partner, and the Foreign and Commonwealth Office, who sent us visitors from zones of religious conflict. We ran a series of 'Springfield Experience' days funded by Tearfund for others setting out on a similar path.

Lest this appears as a self-congratulatory catalogue, it is good both to remember that this can only be God's work, and to shine the hard light of 2023 on those heady days. We well knew of many Christian social enterprises which over time grew larger than the churches which gave them birth and, often though accepting government funding, lost their Christian inspiration. We foresaw the dangers and took what steps seemed open to us to guard against them, and went ahead.

Those who remain at the centre of the Springfield Project today - the trustees, volunteers and workers at the heart of it all - have the responsibility of discerning the paths now open to them. We are now twinned for the delivery of services with a secular project having a different ethos, part of the rationalisation by local government as financial stringency began to bite. Yet in today's fractured world there is still that refreshing sense of welcome and peace as one enters the building, with people of many faiths and cultures sharing and delighting in what can only be seen as a foretaste of the Kingdom.

In 2010 five Springfield Project Topic Sheets were produced for the Springfield Experience Days, run for groups who came from across the country in response to Tearfund's invitation. They are titled *The Purpose of a Christian Community Project*, *Starting Up*,

Relationship between Church and Project, Keeping a Christian Ethos, and *Thinking Through Spiritual Transformation in the Area.*

In the different world of the 2020s we have now hit all the hard questions arising from church involvement with major secular agencies and funders. Yet, in spite of some painful failure we remain committed and in some new ways able to share 'God's Love in our Community'. This can only be God's doing. The beautiful new building was completed and handed to the church at Easter 2008 and formally opened, with the help of some small children, by Archbishop Rowan Williams later in the year. By 2010 we had become a charity, with most of the trustees being church members.

Seedlings remains the one area still led by volunteers, the expanded mums and toddlers group meeting two days a week in the church itself. Cleared of church furniture, the large space is set out with tiny tables and chairs as for a nursery with a variety of toys and equipment laid out ready. By 9.15am a stream of mothers and their little ones would be coming in through the Project entrance, numbers being limited to forty. Grandpas were also eligible along with mainly female volunteers as each one was welcomed.

That the welcome felt everywhere in the Project is so heartwarming is surely due in part to the reality that some of the volunteers, and over time also many employed workers including some now in leadership, had first come for assistance as users at an earlier time of difficulty in their own lives. Whatever their home circumstances, ethnicity or situation, each was known by name, and the atmosphere was happy and purposeful. A quiet buzz of conversation and concentration shared by forty small children and their carers was the norm and still, bar Covid closures, has continued week by week. God's Love in our Community, as the large banner outside the Church proclaimed, was the motto we were seeking to live out.

So, I would sit on a little chair and over time heard some of the mothers' stories. Most were happy enough, with of course the ups and downs of life. In retrospect I think especially of two mothers. One was a Yemeni lady who was brave enough to tell part of her history in 'Our Story So Far' produced for funders in 2010. She had been a pharmacy technician and a social work assistant, but after multiple miscarriages and still births, and suffering post-natal depression, had turned to the Family Support group at the Centre knowing she would find the understanding and kindness needed to help her through a dark tunnel. She had herself gone from referring others for professional help to realising her need to refer herself. When I met her and her one strong little boy in Seedlings

Seedlings.

she was beginning to give back what she had received through contributing at Parents' Voice meetings.

Another was a lady whom I noticed looked sad. I asked her where her family had come from and she told me a little of her story as an Eritrean. She said - this was in 2014 - 'last week three hundred of my people were drowned in the Mediterranean. They were all Catholics.' Memory is fallible. Was it 200 or 400? But it was in the hundreds.

Such were exceptional, but many, from 'hard to reach' local families, had also, far from home, been married very young and lacking English, had found a haven in the Centre. As Estelle Morris, visiting when she was Secretary of State for Education, said, it was 'an oasis'.

Comfortable readers, irrespective of religion or ethnicity, may be helped to enter the scene through this poem by one of our neighbours who for a while was the Children's Centre Teacher.

How Poor is Poor?

How poor is poor?
Can you measure it in pounds?
On the scales of disadvantage
Push life chances to the ground?
Do the scales of disadvantage
Measure levels of exclusion,
Stigmatism, solitude
Isolation and derision?

How poor is poor?
Can you shift the arrow head
From rock bottom to esteem,
To confidence instead?

Is it possible to review
The pointer of despair
Reverse the sloping scale
Reassess what's measured there?

How rich is poor?
There is another scale
To measuring disadvantage
Of those we might deride
There is another measure
A different marked out scale
To assess the worth of those
Disadvantaged, doomed to fail.

How rich is poor?
Can you measure it in caring
Community and kindness
Having nothing yet sharing?

You can measure it in love
Resourcefulness and giving,
Every day full of effort
Just to keep on living.

Julie Afridi Martin

How had all this happened? Like many practical Christian
ventures, it began with a vision. Back around 1980 some older
Christian women prayed, prayed and continued praying that God
would bless the church with children and young people. Even today
there are people in St Christopher's who are sure that without those
women and their prayers the Springfield Project and its various
ministries would never have been born. Seedlings as a mothers'

and toddlers' group had begun in 1988 but it was ten years before it really took off as the vital part (the root) of the tree. The ladies concerned also spoke of Jesus' parable of the tiny mustard seed which grew into the greatest of all the garden plants, so that the birds could shelter in its branches. Thus the Springfield Project came about, a tree with very many branches.

Taking up the vicar's challenge back in 1998 the church followed a well-worn path: a Project subcommittee. We sought and found funding for a feasibility study, asked an architect to draw plans for a grand building, for which we hoped to get European Community funding, then sought funding to appoint a manager. Paul Wrobel came as manager: but no European funding came with him! No big building! And so Paul got busy with a skip and a paintbrush to clean out the old hall and brighten up the place. Cupboards were turned into offices, storerooms into meeting places. Caroline and Sue, dynamic teachers at St John's School, went part time to start a nursery where children could continue after Seedlings. Urgent requests and more fundraising led to the start of Family Support, so by 2002 we had a nursery, a playgroup and family support as well as Seedlings. A Saturday morning Boys Club had started with weekends in Snowdonia and elsewhere, and detached Youth Work with local secondary schools. We began with a Christmas party, then went on, year by year, to add Easter and summer parties.

Confident relationships were growing with several hundred local families. The men folk were in the mosque, while many of the women and children were across the road with us.

We had at the start defined our aims as:

* providing relevant community support in the area of Springfield
* being a community focus open to all

106

* crossing social and cultural barriers;
* networking and collaborating with other agencies
* promoting understanding and the common good
* supporting family relationships

There had followed a discussion to summarise this list into a simple mission statement to express the aim of loving our neighbour. The church was clear; it was not just a hook to attract more Christians. Should we speak of 'Christ's love' or of 'God's love'? As Christians we believe the second is the perfect expression of the first, but so long as Christianity can be seen as an enemy such a sign could be divisive, so we settled on the sign on a large banner which announced: 'God's love in Our Community'.

Funding had been secured for a second three-year term for Paul as project leader. Charities, local and national, were ready to help, the largest being Henry Smith, Esme Fairbairn, the Church Urban Fund and Tearfund. With the coming of Dr Toby Howarth as vicar in 2004, the pace and depth quickened. Yvonne Gordon, a Senior Social Work Trainer, as chair from 2005, somehow (that meant, with Yvonne, with prayer) acted also as manager for two years after Paul's funding ended.

So many things came together. God had placed us at a point in time and space to live out his purposes that we could only partly see, but longed to follow. The reasons for sensing this included 1) our position at a meeting place of cultures, faiths and social classes; and 2) our times - after 9/11 and 7/7, Iraq and Afghanistan. In this setting we continued to feel God's hand at work: he had been progressively showing us his purposes; he had collected in one congregation people with a unique variety of gifts, experience and expertise and had called us together into very diverse ministries with one common purpose: to make his love known. The Springfield Surgery, the Pregnancy Advice Service, the Springfield Project, and many of our members' work situations all shared in this. We had seen increasingly warm personal relations with leading members of the Muslim community at a time when, nationally and city wide, fear and mistrust increasingly marked relations between the Muslim community and all others. We also experienced growing relationships with other churches and with a range of statutory and voluntary agencies including police, education and health services at various levels.

It was with this understanding that the church, with an increasing proportion of our members volunteers or paid workers in the Project, agreed in 2006 at their second invitation to consider the City Council's request to be the Children's Centre for Sparkhill.

We had, a few months earlier, seen that our local mums and toddlers had no qualms about meeting in the church 'under the cross', instead of the 'neutral hall'. We had been hesitant about using the church, but the memorial service for Baksho Chamber, our much-loved Punjabi Christian worker, brought everyone together there.

In starting to think about the City's proposal, at first we said, 'We don't have space.' They said, 'We can build it for you.'

And so began an astonishing process, marked by goodwill and manifest trust on all sides, as we in the church, supported by the Diocese, wrestled with matters of principle, legality and finance over issues as varied as our Christian basis, losing the church hall, and the construction and ownership of the new building. City officers in the education, planning, architects and legal departments sought to answer our queries.

Children's Centres provided for families and children under five years, but we also wanted provision in a new building for Youth Work, evening meetings and Sunday School, for cross-cultural and Faith to Faith work and training, and for office space for all of this. In the end the City made a little over £2 million available and the church raised a further £140,000. The church was to run the Children's Centre, so long as funding was continued, for twenty-five years. The City made revenue funding available well before the legal agreement had been finalised. First we were able to appoint Michelle as manager in 2006, and a year later could appoint a Centre Director.

That we were thinking beyond local level was clear from the advertisement placed in *The Guardian* with its strapline, 'Can you keep the kids in play-dough while having tea with an African Archbishop and an Imam?' This scenario had in fact occurred a little earlier when those dignitaries, at the Foreign and Commonwealth Office's instigation, had visited us and the Woodlands Road Mosque. The advertisement caught the interest of Angie King who had run Sure Start Children's Centres for the Council and was taking a year out for Bible College. Her years with the Project were just one more touch of God's bringing the people he wanted at the right time.

Seen in retrospect, the appointment by Bishop Sentamu of Dr Toby Howarth as vicar and then as his Interfaith Advisor was significant, with his influence ranging from Woodlands Road Mosque to the FCO.

Good things continued and in 2023 still continue. In 2007 Dr and Mrs Andrew Smith joined St Christopher's, setting up Youth Encounter and then The Feast, both initially based in the Centre. Dr and Mrs Richard Sudworth have also come and stayed, with Richard following Toby as the Archbishop's Interfaith Advisor at Lambeth but worshipping with us. We may grow weary, but God does not.

Equally vital in God's eyes for sure and also now in the joyful membership of the church and its outreach into the Project through Seedlings and otherwise, are several saints whose earlier lives were more marked by distress and difficulty and who now play their vital part in a live and life-giving church. Significantly the church also includes former Sikh and Hindu members, but not at the time of writing Muslim. They share much of the Punjabi language and the North Indian culture of those the Project mainly serves. Slowly but surely, St Christopher's becomes truly multicultural. Like the Church everywhere in this world we are still 'work in progress', but there is enough to hold the vision of black, brown and white, young and old, male and female, singing God's praise in life as in worship together.

As surely in many places, no list can fully convey the sense that God has been bringing the people he wants for particular service at particular times, and that we are collected for a purpose we can only glimpse and whose fulfilment can only be understood in the sense of the prayer 'Thy kingdom come on earth...'

In worldly terms, the vital national importance of good and mutually honest relationships between the Muslim community and wider British society needs no underlining. One thing I was taught through participating in the scene at Springfield for twenty years was that it is better to light a candle than to curse the darkness. If such candles can be multiplied, it will be better for us all.

BACK TO SCHOOL

Golden Hillock

Most of my life had been 'school': a wartime boyhood cycling five miles each way to Caterham; a totally unforeseen and deeply formative first employment at Gordonstoun; a life changing exposure to so different a culture at Lawrence College in Pakistan; and then, again unforeseen, the invitation to lead the Tyndale Biscoe School in the centre of Srinagar: a deep immersion in local society in the leading city High School whose founder was described in public by the Chief Minister of the State as the founder of modern Kashmir.

Thus, landing from the outer cultural space of Srinagar into Sparkhill in April 1987 and seeing the children walking along Golden Hillock Road to the school within earshot of our temporary home, it seemed the obvious thing to go along and say hello to Mrs Stirling Stewart the Head Teacher. She had worked in Africa, and indeed returned to Malawi after leaving Golden Hillock, and was glad to see someone who enthused about her school. She asked if I would be happy to be co-opted on to the Governing Body, and so began a long and, for twenty years, happy association. A further few years, less happy and meriting further reflection, followed on.

An 11 to 16 mixed comprehensive with about 900 children, it always felt welcoming. Brisk but smiling, whether it was the student on duty at the door, the caretaker or a teacher, it had the 'feel' of a good school. I steadily came to know its workings, and became chair about the time that Thelma Probert became headteacher in 1998. It was her twelve-year leadership that marked the school with real distinction.

The majority of the children were Pakistani Mirpuris, with grandparents and very often mothers from that little knot of villages in the Punjabi-Pahari speaking fringe on the western side of what had been the Dogra Maharajah's princely state of Kashmir. As so often with that age group, the girls seemed quite dominant, worked harder than the boys and were cleverer at navigating life between two cultures.

English had been the playground language until very recently, according to my neighbour and fellow governor Javed, who had studied in the school a few years earlier when it was more truly multicultural, but the Mirpuri variant of Punjabi had taken over since then. Although about a fifth of the children were Sylhetti speakers from northern Bangladesh there was no doubting the dominant culture.

Some of the older teachers looked back to the time when the school's make-up was still largely English, with the boys going on to work in the factories of Tyseley. The factories had closed in the 1980s and apart from taxi driving and the corner shop, work was hard to find. I suspect some of the staff lacked appreciation of the determination to succeed which marks most immigrant communities. Running counter to parents' high expectations of the school was a cultural expectation that the girls did household chores while their brothers ran free.

Miss Thelma Probert OBE was part of the invaluable Welsh mafia among head teachers in Birmingham. Next to coal, teachers had been the main export from the Welsh Valleys to England. I had benefited from several, both at primary and secondary level, in my schooldays before and during the Second World War. As one of a minority herself and as a female head, Miss Probert used her skills for the great good of all. The school felt like a community, down to the humblest kitchen assistant or the neglected child; all this with a warm practical humanity. She knew that whereas the boys had it easy at home, the girls in many families would have to help prepare the food in a joint family, then clean the pots before starting their homework.

Most of the children lived close by. The best teachers knew the kids in their classes, with home visiting when needed, rather to my surprise. Thelma, finding a Bengali girl in tears, learned that she needed fostering. Social services, unable to place her with a Bengali home, had put her with a Pakistani couple whose home language was incomprehensible to her, and she was being used as a servant by a professional couple who said she was lucky to be with them. Given the recent history of the two countries it was not surprising. Appealing to Thelma she said, if not Bengali she would be happy with an English or Caribbean family where she could understand what they said. Thelma won her battle, as she usually did, and all went well.

A woman head was well placed to deal with other tricky situations, such as if a girl said her religion didn't allow swimming. She would check with the mosque, then take the girl's mother along to the nearby pool for her to see it was 'women only'. She was also at an advantage in dealing with the *biraderi* elder who was somewhat lost when dealing with a woman in authority.

Though only just over two miles from the city centre, many of the children - especially the girls - never went there. The school did all it could to widen their horizon whether in visits to the Council Chamber or to an art gallery or for weekends in the Outdoor Centre in North Wales or day trips in the Shropshire hills.

Cricket, even played with sticks for stumps on a patch of grass at the Ackers ground just up the road, was a passion especially when the Pakistani team was at Edgbaston. It was Frank, our caretaker from the Caribbean and himself a devotee, who coached the school team. Tim Boyes, who came to Golden Hillock as a young Senior Teacher, was a charismatic drama teacher. On one occasion I was showing some guests around, and had warned Tim. Approaching the Hall there was a lot of shouting and I could see the important visitors shaking their heads as if to confirm their fears about 'bog standard comprehensives'. As we went in the drama came to its climax, the scene of a family row. The children had learned that their uncle had been 'doing drugs' - trading in them. The dilemma was whether to report him or not, with passionate arguments both ways. The visitors were impressed.

We invited everyone along. Professor Tim Brighouse was to come to Birmingham as CEO. Thelma had called a community meeting after a television programme had stirred up strong feeling locally. I cheekily contacted Tim and invited him to attend. Ten minutes into a lively meeting he sidled in, rather like an ageing hippie, whispering, 'I'm Tim,' and sat, following closely. As CEO he was known to turn up in a staffroom at 8am with chocolates or a bottle of sherry, knowing he would find a gang of teachers hard at work.

Estelle Morris, a Coventry humanities teacher herself, became MP for neighbouring Yardley, and we asked her to visit both then and again later as Secretary of State for Education. She was surely the only Cabinet member ever whose resignation was greeted with tears by a conference of headteachers, as happened when she announced it to them.

At least three of our staff went on to headships in the City, joining a very confident group over that period. They were a close-knit fellowship, not too bothered by prevailing guidance over recruitment, phoning friends to get the lowdown on an applicant. The teaching vocation was just too important to be hamstrung by politically correct bureaucracy.

The Runnymede Trust had circulated a consultation paper on Islamophobia to which a Muslim teacher and I replied, as did two year seven children with whom the head had discussed it, our responses being quoted in its final Report. The following are excerpts.

> Dear Runnymede Trust, My name is … and I am thirteen years old. I am a British Muslim. I think I am very fortunate to be able to come to a mixed community school where the majority of the pupils are Muslim. The staff understand and respect the needs of their pupils and try to help us as far as possible. I am writing to invite you to come and have a look at our school…

From the same class came this. 'I'm a Hindu boy in Golden Hillock School and my name is…, and I think the school is doing more than enough for Muslims, because the Muslim rate is higher. It doesn't matter if your religion is fewer… every religion should be treated fairly because we're all human…'

The teacher listed ways in which pupils' cultural and pastoral needs were met, and I was quoted as follows: 'Teachers who are willing to adapt to change and who have natural sympathy with a child who has extra hoops to jump through, tend to choose inner city schools. Such sensitive teachers are often children's best friends. The children are growing into a world where they will be both Pakistani/Sylhetti and British. Their homes and communities prepare them for the former, their teachers for the latter. With Arabic learned at Quran lessons, they just grow up trilingual. Teachers who listen to children, and head teachers who support them, are the most vital resource.' Again, the chief role of a Chair of Governors was to support a good headteacher.

Thelma was wise in dealing with religious questions. Like most schools with large Muslim intakes we sidestepped the requirement to hold daily 'mainly and broadly Christian worship' in assembly. Indeed in 1995 it was reckoned that 95 per cent of schools across the country avoided this almost unworkable provision. Nor did we ask for a 'determination'. We simply praised good work in assembly, made necessary announcements, and from time to time welcomed a former student who had done well to give some encouragement. In Assembly as at other formal occasions, pin drop silence was expected and given.

Unlike her predecessor, Thelma accepted the request for those who wished to join Friday prayers, and thus a modest change was made in the timetable. In the event, few attended the prayers, but it is wise to know which battles are worth fighting.

Governors were mainly very local parents and community members, concerned citizens of good common sense. Most were naturally Pakistani and Muslim except for the teacher governors and one or two like Mrs Lynn Morris CBE, for long the distinguished Principal of Joseph Chamberlain College, the next stage for many of our children. We also included a Muslim lady GP who advised on sex education in a very matter of fact way and a Tesco manager who sometimes brought delicious sandwiches or eclairs to cheer our lengthy meetings. We were very aware of the need for more Asian or Muslim teachers, but few offered for interview. School teaching was not, it seemed, a profession of choice for men in the community, and the few good Asian teachers we did have were mainly Hindu or Sikh, and mainly women.

We were able to attract some valuable volunteers, outstanding among them being Val from Knowle Parish Church. She was a nurse, and so useful and popular that when a classroom assistant's post came up the head suggested she apply for it. To quote her, 'As soon as I entered this lovely warm school it felt like coming home; the children are so friendly to all. Even passing the OFSTED inspectors in the corridors they'd say "Hi! How are you doing?

Can I help?"' She knew she'd like to stay. As a nurse (the school doesn't officially have one) it's usually a little TLC that's needed for the common minor sicknesses or sports injuries. This may involve taking children to their homes and explaining their needs to their mothers. Many of the girls come in and share their problems. She led a parenting group and - boys included - called it a babysitting class. The school has physically disabled children, which brings out the caring best in their classmates. A sad sequel was that Val's 18-year-old daughter who would sometimes come in too and became much loved, then succumbed to leukaemia and died. It was most moving to see several hundred of our girls coming by coach for her funeral in Knowle's ancient village church.

Was it a kinder, less fiercely competitive age? In some ways, yes. But the head was very clear on professional standards. We slowly climbed the proportion of those getting at least the five A to C grades in GCSE, with students who had come into year seven well behind the national average and of course with most of them having English as a second or third language. We also gave prominence to drama and music, both hugely popular, to give as rounded an education as possible. It was one of my larger privileges, as Chair of Governors, to be her 'critical friend'. When we first met, perhaps alarmed by my occasional clerical collar, she said, 'I'm afraid you won't think me much of a Christian. My father became a communist because the chapels weren't caring for the miners in the injustices they were suffering.' My reflection was of the tragedy for church and nation of the split between evangelicalism and social action.

Sometime in the 1990s a grant was received for creative writing, and the school published a booklet of illustrations and stories entitled *Izzat Zarruri Hai*, 'Honour is Essential'. The following is one of the more modest offerings printed.

117

Misunderstanding

Shaida walked slowly down Golden Hillock Road, deliberately taking her time. She knew that she was in deep trouble. She knew that her parents were old fashioned and what their response would be when they were told what she had done that day.

Of all the teachers in the School, the teacher who thought a lot of her had to catch her out. She admired Miss Halsall, and knew that the fact she was caught playing truant from School would ruin their relationship. And the fact that she was with a boy! Her parents might cope with the truancy but when they found out that it was with one of her friends, a boy, they would be really mad.

She thought of all the things that might happen to her and at one time she thought that she might even be sent back to Pakistan. When she finally got home, she took a deep breath and opened the door with her key.

She breathed a sigh of relief; Miss Halsall hadn't arrived yet. Instead she saw her uncle. Her parents respected her uncle and listened to him a lot. Almost immediately there was a knock at the door and she went to go to her room.

"Where are you going?" asked her mother. "Don't you want to talk to your uncle?"

She hesitated for a moment, knowing that if she didn't talk to her uncle they would think that something was wrong. She always talked with her uncle, she found him very interesting. She quickly replied, "I've got a lot of homework" and ran upstairs.

She sat upstairs in her room, very worried. She heard the front door open and close. Then she could hear Miss Halsall's voice, and even make out some of the things that were being said about her. "Your daughter is a very bright girl who should do well in her exams if she doesn't play truant from school with boys."

There was a brief pause, then her father shouted, "*Jaldi neeche au!*"

She panicked and knew what would happen next. Her father's voice became louder as he repeated himself, "*Jaldi neeche au!*"

She walked down slowly, hearing only the traffic outside. As she reached the bottom of the stairs she saw the expressions on her parents' faces.

"*Ye sach hai he him ne yen liegun hai?*" her mother asked.

Miss Halsall, knowing it would be a family discussion, said, "I must be going."

"Thank you for letting us know," said Shaida's mother politely.

After Miss Halsall had left there was a moment of silence before her father spoke. "You're a Muslim girl and you know you're not supposed to go out with boys and you know how I feel about this whole topic." His voice was quiet and it seemed as if he was trying to keep his anger under control to stop himself from exploding.

"You know what I should do with you. You know ... well, I'll tell you. You're going back to Pakistan to live with your brother. He'll put you back where you belong. Now go to your room."

Back in her room she could hear her parents talking. She was thinking of running away and then she heard her parents shouting. Her mother seemed to be on her side, she could hear her say, "You had no right to make a decision like that. I know she should be punished but that was going too far." Then there was more discussion which she couldn't make out. A period of silence followed before she heard her uncle say, "Stop arguing. You don't even know what she has to say. You're no longer in Pakistan now. Times have changed." Minutes later, she heard the door open and close, and she realised he had gone. There was no more shouting and her parents seemed to be talking quietly.

"Come down," her father called up to her. When she came down, he told her, "You tell us what happened."

"Well I wagged school and went to the park where Jabber was also wagging school so I decided to stay with him and then Miss Halsall came and caught us."

"Okay, we believe you. We think you should be punished for wagging school and we are sorry for the misunderstanding. But I am very strongly against you having a boyfriend."

"But I haven't got one," replied Shaida angrily. knowing her father did not like being answered back.

Her mother quickly said, "We know you haven't got a boyfriend and we don't want you to have a boyfriend. If you disobey us we'll have to take precautions."

"No boyfriends," her father said firmly.

GLOSSARY

Jaldi niche au	Come down quickly
Ye sach hai he hin yen lien hai?	Is this true what I hear?

Such a simple story speaks volumes about culture, then and even now. It may be a good bridge to the even more complicated scene of 2023. Though the period was for most schools in Birmingham a hopeful time and though Golden Hillock was untroubled and confident, some schools in the City were not. For Golden Hillock too there was major difficulty ahead, bursting into public view in *The Sunday Times* in 2014 and rumbling on eight years later thanks to the publicity given by podcasts sponsored by *The New York Times*.

Even so, it is hard to end this chapter, reflecting the dedicated work of many teachers, and of many others in building positive community relationships, with the note that follows.

The Trojan Horse

It was as world-wide dramatic headlines charted the rise of Islamic State that a story emerged about extremists taking over Birmingham schools. Even ten years later, there tend to be separate views, right- or left-wing or liberal-intellectual, all showing little understanding as to how Islamism works. Over more than a decade, in a number of schools where most pupils were Muslim Pakistanis, small groups of governors responded very differently to a covert Islamist policy leadership. Such policy was unstated, and covered by very convincing and reasonable pressure for largely agreed goals, such as fuller sharing in leadership decision-making from minority groups.

Every Governors' meeting became a struggle, cooperation withered and several good headteachers, including our own from Golden Hillock, were forced into resignation. In 2024, in an age of cancel culture, it belongs to the past and is best left there. The 'Trojan Horse' document itself, an unsigned 'letter' dropped on to the desk of the City Council leader - and when he didn't sufficiently respond, given to the *Sunday Times* - was a deadly shaft. Purportedly an encouragement to a Muslim 'Brother' in Bradford to repeat there the success in taking over Birmingham schools, naming accurately the steps needed to bring down an unsympathetic headteacher, it was perhaps written by a disillusioned sister aiming her dart at the Chair of the Park View Trust.

Be that as it may, it fed into a wider atmosphere where 'Islamic plot' was all too easily believed. The 2022 attempt to reverse the story, publicised by *The New York Times*' podcasts, attracted only limited attention, but was a reminder that grievance always thrives on both real and perceived injustice.

As someone inevitably involved in the unhappy saga, and reflecting on Kashmir experience, I was surprised that none of the commentators spoke of the covert Islamism which was a core aspect of the policy of PVET, the Park View Educational Trust, hidden even from well-meaning trustees.

In the complex 'equalities' scene in Birmingham today, when social media is so dominant that unidentified people can slander and drag anyone's name through the mud while remaining invisible, it serves no helpful purpose to rehearse the damaging affair.

In issues in the public sphere where strong differences are to be expected, the philosopher John Gray offers practical wisdom. He wrote the following in *Enlightenment's Wake* as long ago as 1995:

> A stable liberal society cannot be radically multi-cultural, but depends for its successful renewal across the generations on an undergirding culture that is held in common. This common culture need not encompass a shared religion that is held in common, but it does demand certain norms and conventions of behaviour ... in the British case vague but still powerful notions of give and take, of the necessity of compromise and of not imposing private convictions on others, are elements of what is left of the common culture, and they are essential if a liberal civil society is to survive in Britain ...c entral are freedom of expression and its precondition, the rule of law.

When we arrived in Sparkhill in 1987, I still harboured the thought that 'it's all about Muslims'. Long before we left to live close to family in virtually all English and all white East Yorkshire in 2014, I knew it was, much more about the West as it now is and about God's Church worldwide, the place of confident hope where he is building his Kingdom.

HOPE IN 2023

It is only since leaving Birmingham in 2014 that there has been leisure to reflect. Equally it is only in these last years that some of the bad fruit of the 1960s has begun to be so evident, with the insecurities and blows of Covid 19 and climate change ever more threatening, accentuated by the self-inflicted damage of Brexit.

Our Birmingham years were as fulfilling, happy and packed with incident as those in Kashmir. In British society the constant has appeared to be the triumphant progress of materialism, yet at the same time strong currents of hope have persisted and grown in the Church and more widely.

When we arrived in Birmingham I was still confused about the nature of mission in the British multicultural setting, though we were surely guided to St John's. Early on, setting up the 'St John's Occasional Meetings', we had asked Lesslie Newbigin to speak on 'Evangelism in Multicultural Birmingham'. He seemed surprised as well as pleased to meet a group of mainly young Christians who actually expected people to turn to Christ. With his wonderfully youthful mien in his eighties, this theologian missionary bishop who has been referred to as 'reminiscent of one of the early fathers of the Church', in pastoring the small URC congregation in Winson Green became an inspiration, model and friend to many.

At the time I still thought in terms of mission to Muslims, but by the time we left in 2014 I was convinced that 'the number one question for us', by far the deepest missionary challenge, as Lesslie had seen much earlier, is whether the West can be converted. I had also found in practice that the place where we can best put in our pennyworth is the community of the local Church. Deeply prophetic, he suggested forty years ago conditions for the Church to begin to face such a challenge to our collapsed pagan culture in the public sphere: to critically examine the totality of things as our whole culture understands them from within the framework of Scripture and the tradition of Christian thought. It is to consider such a challenge that this book will end, but regarding Islam, Birmingham taught me that, though a godless society may well fear Islam in its midst, those hoping to share the Gospel find that any such fear is replaced by love just so far as God's Spirit is allowed to rule our hearts, minds and actions. Beyond this we can be encouraged by the reality that, in Britain as elsewhere, God himself is at work bringing Muslims, like others of every creed and culture who are willing to suffer for him, into the vast multitude which no one can number described in Revelation chapter seven. Just occasionally, he allows us glimpses into what he is doing. The question is whether we have eyes to see and ears to hear what is happening, and whether the Church can be formed anew in flexibility and imagination in its structures to make use of the newcomers' gifts and calling.

Of those we count among close friends are a few who have made that extraordinary journey from Islam to Christ. Two in particular, seeking theological education would have naturally found it within the Church of England. One was recommended for and began theological training with the note that he was called to a 'workplace ministry'. It transpired that his vision was too daring for inclusion within the system, however. He is now serving Christ as a much-valued advisor in a sensitive area of national policy, though not in the UK. The other was snapped up by a different church, not quite 'mainstream' but truly spreading the Gospel. It offered both theological training and an entry to the ministry to which she is surely called, of evangelism and discipling women of her own Pakistani culture in congregations across London. I had earlier enquired of the Bishop of Chelmsford[16] as to possibilities within the Church of England, but was told that the route to training is normally through the applicant's home congregation. Only converts from Islam usually do not have one.

Islam in Britain of course remains a large factor, whether in mission or in secular, intellectual and political terms, in that it provides a coherent and clamant alternative model of society, attractive to some, perhaps to many, in a rootless and fast changing culture.

In terms of Christian mission it is like a large rock placed in the road ahead. Others before Newbigin had raised the spectre of an even bigger adversary facing us, something far stronger even than Islam. Dostoevsky, writing of the 'national apostasy' he found in nineteenth-century Europe, and Meissner and others seeing the weakness of the German Church in the 1930s, posed to the next generation this real Number One Question, the immense boulder field of our own culture. Can the West be converted? Newbigin confessed he did not know the answer, but he suggested guidelines for this 'far more difficult mission field'. A summary of them detailed in his *Mission and the Crisis of Western Culture* still calls aloud for the priority it requires, and is the proper conclusion of this book.

He cites six areas of the scale of change needed by the Church in the West where 'Christianity' is confined to the personal sphere and our public life is ruled by beliefs that are false.

1. A serious challenge would entail the de-clericalising of the Church. We must learn to 'do religion' in the public sphere: in the daily business of governments, trade unions, transnational corporations, universities and schools.

---

16 Rt Revd Guli Dehqani Tafti.

2. The apocalyptic strand of New Testament teaching, without which there is no hope for the world, is to be recovered.

3. We need a doctrine of freedom resting not on Enlightenment ideology, but on the Gospel itself. We cannot say that until we can show that we have learned the lesson that we understand the difference between bearing witness to the truth and pretending to possess it. Such witness requires not dominance but suffering.

4. A radical break with denominationalism: 'the visible form of a surrender to our culture'.

5. Listening to the witness of Christians from other cultures. This is a great new asset; we need, and can have, their eyes to see ourselves.

6. A fundamental: courage. 'Our wrestling is not with flesh and blood but with principalities and powers.' Aligned with Paul, we need to speak, 'taking every thought captive to Christ.' For that we need more than the weapons of this world.

Newbigin's summary surely was prophetic back in the 1980s. None of the cultural, social or political developments since then have lessened the force of such assertion.

This book has been autobiographical. Scripture says, 'Here we have no continuing city, but we seek a city to come.' That could be a fitting note on which to conclude, seeking hope for generations to come, but this book has touched on a long life journey through education and culture as well as faith.

Christian faith remains after two thousand years the best guide to loving God and loving one's neighbour - or else it is of little benefit. Its contexts and challenges change but God's love, to which it is the response, does not. Culture and education - prime aspects of life as we humans have experienced it over time and space – do, however, change, and never more so than in my generation which now has unlimited power, for good or ill, whether for travel to distant space, or for the destruction of the earth upon which we live. The world's leading scientists describe our techno-industrial culture as fundamentally dysfunctional, systematically consuming the biophysical basis of its own existence. They also conclude, however, that technically it is entirely possible, if we had a coherent, integrated approach worldwide, that it would 'not be beyond us to transition to clean energy, develop a sustainable food system, and all the rest of it.'[17]

It is thus to a deep change of values, and the thinking, actions and policies that spring from them, that mankind must urgently look. Where else can he hope to find them other than in the Church as it can be, reflecting not only God's love and purpose for the souls of man, but for the perfection of His beautiful, created world? As I near the end of my journey touched by grace these many years, that is my hope for my grandchildren.

---

17 Mike Berners-Lee, *There is No Planet B: A Handbook for the Make or Break Years*, Cambridge: Cambridge University Press, 2019.